College Style Sheet

USA EDITION

Jon Furberg
&
Richard Hopkins

BENDALL BOOKS
MILL BAY • POINT ROBERTS

BENDALL BOOKS
U.S. address: 1574 Gulf Road, Box 361, Point Roberts, Washington 98281
Canadian address: Box 115, Mill Bay, British Columbia V0R 2P0

College Style Sheet, *USA Edition*
Copyright © 1993 by Jon Furberg and Richard Hopkins.
All rights reserved.

Published by special arrangement with Vancouver Community College Press.
Material from *A Casebook of Ideologies* by Macdonald Burbidge © 1990 reprinted
with permission of VCC Press. Sample essay pages reproduced with permission
of Leslie Peeler, Jeff Webster, and Tim Hopkins.

Printed in Canada
97 96 95 94   5 4 3

CATALOGING IN PUBLICATION DATA
Furberg, Jon, 1944-1992.
College style sheet

ISBN0-9696985-0-X
Includes index.
1. Report writing.   2. English language—Rhetoric
I. Hopkins, Richard, 1936- .   II. Title
PE1408.F87 1993   808'.02   C93-091237-3

Jon Furberg
1944-1992

Contents

Preface and Acknowledgments

This US edition of the *College Style Sheet* mirrors changes made to the third Canadian edition which offers several new and revised sections that reflect current standards and practices.

New are units on APA (American Psychological Association) style, documenting research in Sociology and Biology, nondiscriminatory language, paraphrase, and summary. Also new are common proofreading marks, comments on the use of word processors—and an index.

The following parts have been significantly revised, usually by offering more generous explanation and examples: "Avoiding Plagiarism"; "The Note Style of Documentation"; quoting prose, poetry, and drama; model pages illustrating principal documentation styles; and the section giving sample citations, particularly for government publications.

*　　*　　*

Langara Style Sheet was the heading on a single sheet of paper composed in 1974 by Alan Dawe, of the English department at Vancouver Community College's Langara campus, as a bare-bones documentation guide for students. Suggestions by students and faculty inspired its development into a pamphlet. By 1983, it was widely used in colleges in British Columbia, and the name *College Style Sheet* was adopted. In the mid 1980s, departments other than English were offering descriptions of the documentation styles of their respective disciplines; major changes were announced by the most influential arbiter of style, the Modern Language Association (MLA); moreover, several important aspects of style, such as the use of quotations and references, deserved more attention—all these were addressed in the 1988 edition. Throughout, we have tried to maintain the original spirit of brevity and simplicity.

The *College Style Sheet* is guided in general by the standards of documentation presented by Joseph Gibaldi and Walter S. Achtert in the current edition of their *MLA Handbook for Writers of Research Papers*. We have also consulted the guidelines offered by other pertinent texts listed below under "Standards of Style."

More personally, we are grateful to some fifty semesters of first- and second-year students, whose curses and praises of former editions we have taken to heart. We also wish to thank our colleagues and students at Langara for helpful suggestions and contributions that they might find incorporated here, more or less intact.

Most particularly I am indebted to Jon Furberg, my colleague and friend, whose recent passing still seems unbelievable. Jon, a lover of life and literature, was a remarkable teacher, and his contribution to this work simply cannot be calculated. The *College Style Sheet* stands as a testament to his dedication to his teaching, and to his students.

Richard Hopkins
English Department,
Vancouver Community College,
Langara Campus
February 1993

Introduction

The *College Style Sheet* is not a composition text or a handbook of grammar, punctuation, and usage; it is a guide to help you present essays—especially research essays—according to current conventions of physical layout and documentation of sources. All assignments requiring a paper in which you make use of someone else's words, ideas, or data also require that you acknowledge both your sources and your specific use of them.

Each discipline, or field of study, follows a particular system, or "style," for presenting research material and for directing the reader to the original location of this information. Careful study and imitation of the appropriate conventions outlined here will save you hours of trial and error, and should result in improved grades.

This style guide incorporates, with a few modifications, the current (1988) documentation system defined by the Modern Language Association (MLA) which advocates *text references* and a list of *works cited* for the acknowledgment of sources in essay writing. The MLA system is standard for English and other humanities courses.

Some frequently used terms need clarification. The word *style* signifies the way source material is presented and documented; it does not refer to the quality of your expression. By style is meant the accepted conventions regarding the form and placement of quotations, references to sources (whether summarized, paraphrased, or quoted), works cited (bibliographies), page layout and numbering, title pages, and the like.

The word *text* means the body of your essay (your sentences) including quotations and parenthetical references. A *reference* is the specific acknowledgment of your use of an external source of information; it may appear directly in your sentence or indirectly in a parenthesis, footnote, or endnote. The purpose of a reference is to direct the reader to a corresponding citation.

A *citation* is the full, formal statement of the publishing details for each source. Citations appear in alphabetical order in a list called "Works Cited" at the end of the essay.

This guide also describes the note style (often required for History papers) and the APA style required for Psychology papers. Variants of APA style are used for other social sciences (e.g., Sociology) and some physical sciences (e.g., Biology)—these are also discussed here.

Remember that when your essay makes any use of secondary material, you are "doing research," and conventions govern the way you should acknowledge it. Ask each of your instructors which pages of the *Style Sheet* are pertinent to his or her assignments. Some may not express a preference for one style

1

over another; nevertheless, you must choose one and be consistent. Do not attempt to invent your own. Treat your essay as though you were offering it for publication.

Standards of Style

Academic disciplines rely upon certain standard manuals for models that demonstrate the accepted form of quotations, references, and source citations.

English

After 1984, English faculties began to abandon footnotes and bibliography in favor of the parenthetical references and list of works cited recommended by the MLA. The *College Style Sheet* summarizes the main features of this style. For a full discussion, consult:

> Gibaldi, Joseph, and Walter S. Achtert. <u>MLA Handbook for Writers of Research Papers</u>. 3rd ed. New York: Modern Language Assn. of America, 1988.

This work should be available for quick reference at the reference desk of your campus library, on short-term loan at the reserve desk, or for sale in the campus bookstore.

History and Political Science

These disciplines have tended to retain the traditional footnote style, with some modern variations. The MLA offers its own version of conventions for note style, but for many academics the basic text is still "Turabian":

> Turabian, Kate L. <u>A Manual for Writers of Term Papers, Theses, and Dissertations</u>. 5th ed. Chicago: University of Chicago Press, 1987.

This text should be available at the library reference desk and in the campus bookstore. The note style is discussed on pages 62-67 of this *Sheet*.

Psychology

Psychology papers employ a system of parenthetical references that stress author and date. The style authority is:

American Psychological Association. <u>Publication Manual of the American Psychological Association</u>. 3rd ed. Washington, DC: American Psychological Assn., 1983.

The rudiments of APA style are presented in this *Sheet* (see pages 56-61) together with a sample page and list of works cited. For further information, consult your reference librarian.

Sociology and Biology

Both disciplines use variations of basic APA style, and are illustrated here (see pages 56-61) with examples and notes on distinguishing features.

Nonprint Sources

The *MLA Handbook* and Turabian describe the citing of audio-visual (e.g., films and records), oral (e.g., speeches, lectures, interviews), manuscript (e.g., unpublished works), and microform sources. An even more elaborate set of conventions is available in:

Fleischer, Eugene B. <u>A Style Manual for Citing Microform and Nonprint Media</u>. Chicago: American Library Assn., 1978.

Types of Essays

Before beginning a writing assignment, determine what *type* of essay you are expected to produce. Make sure you know the desired length and scope of the essay, and stick to the limits imposed by your instructor. Does the essay require quotations and references? Should it merely report existing information and ideas? Or are you to offer a *thesis* of your own—the key idea you set out to claim and support by using examples, logically developed arguments, and often research material as well?

Except where noted below, avoid the first-person pronoun, "I," in your essays. Any sentence can be rewritten to remove the self-conscious "I," "me," "my," "mine." It is not necessary to write, "In my opinion," "I believe," "I feel," etc., since the reader assumes your authorship. Similarly, it is redundant, and dull, to begin an essay with a statement of intention such as, "In the following essay, I shall try to prove. . . . "

Personal Experience Essay

In some courses, you may be asked to narrate an event in your life that illustrates a significant truth you have discovered. Write from a first-person point of view (using "I," "me," etc.), and employ vivid sensory language to help draw your reader into the scene. Dialogue is often a valuable means of dramatizing your story; if you use dialogue, imitate the conventions of paragraphing, punctuation, and quotation employed in published short stories or novels.

Expository Essay

A common assignment in many introductory English courses is a short expository essay (about five paragraphs, 350-600 words) in which you either offer information or explain your point of view on a topic you already know about.

These two general kinds of exposition vary according to your intention. One mainly gives information ("Why People Pray"); the other mainly defends an opinion ("Why Prayer Should [or Should Not] Be Permitted in Public Schools"). Here, the intent of each essay is obvious from its title (they could easily be combined to form a longer essay).

Typically, the short expository essay begins with a paragraph that announces the *topic* (subject matter) and builds to a *thesis statement* in which you state your point of view. Then follows the middle portion of your text, consisting of three or more paragraphs of supporting evidence and reasoned discussion based *mainly* on your personal knowledge, experience, and judgment (but not necessarily excluding material from secondary sources). The essay ends with a paragraph that restates the thesis more emphatically and possibly suggests wider implications. A good ending does not merely summarize.

Research Essay

Unlike the expository essay, a research essay *must* present information and ideas gathered from a variety of sources outside your own experience and knowledge. You must consult and use other people's work. In some sense, all learning is the product of research: our understanding of the world develops and changes as we talk with others, read newspapers, magazines, and books, watch films and television, and observe and react to events around us. When we want to know the answer to an important question, we often find we have to seek help in a source outside ourselves.

In a formal research essay, you must offer a well-developed thesis supported by convincing evidence and opinion found in appropriate sources that are referred to in your text and given credit with full citations in a list of works cited at the end.

Basically, there are two kinds of research. "Primary research" generates new or up-to-date information from interviews, experiments, surveys, or other direct observations. When you are asked to view a painting or read a short story or poem, and then to give your ideas or interpretation, you are also doing primary research—the particular work directly before you provides your sole source of evidence for making your judgment.

"Secondary research" relies upon already published information and ideas found mainly in libraries—in books, scholarly journals, magazines, audiotapes, videotapes, microforms, and so on. Although many assignments require secondary (library) research alone, some combine the two kinds.

Through research you enlarge your knowledge and understanding of a subject and thus your capacity to draw intelligent, forceful conclusions. Some assignments ask only that you prove you have understood a problem; others, that you commit yourself to a solution.

Research essays regularly employ quotation (also paraphrase and summary), text references (or notes), and a list of works cited. Sometimes other aids such as graphs, tables, and diagrams are helpful. Your research, from a *variety* of reliable sources (one or two are insufficient), must be incorporated logically as the essay develops. The key is to keep your thesis in mind always. What are you trying to prove? What are you trying to illustrate?

Try to find sources that are authoritative whenever you do research—some instructors will turn to your list of works cited, to see how current and full your research has been, even before they read your text.

Literary Insight Essay

English courses in short fiction, poetry, drama, film, and the novel require papers in which you interpret, and perhaps evaluate, a work of literary or cinematic art. There are several ways you can read and meaningfully discuss a work of literature or any other art form: (1) as a created thing, interesting in itself; (2) as a mirror of significant truths about the external world; (3) as a stimulus that calls forth inner feelings and self-awareness; and (4) as the expression of an artist with unique skills, intelligence, and character.

Your instructor may ask only for a personal interpretation of the work at hand. In this case, you are doing primary research; the essay offers your own "insight" without reference to published criticism. You should summarize, paraphrase, and quote the literary text with sufficient frequency to illustrate the key points of your analysis. In-class essay tests are of this kind, as are some home papers. Remember that *your insight is your thesis*.

Term papers, however, usually require that you do secondary research—finding agreement, controversy, and radically different approaches to the same work or author to provide support for your own point of view. By consulting, citing, and quoting pertinent critical works in the library, you give the essay greater authority.

Technical Essay

Science courses sometimes require essays in which you record observations, experiments, data, etc., to illustrate your understanding of a particular scientific principle. You may have to describe a procedure, explain a law, or define a certain term.

Research Report

Research reports and research essays share a common purpose—to present the reader with interesting and useful information drawn from primary and/or secondary sources. But whereas essays are intended mainly for a general audience, reports, being more "technical," are aimed at a more specific, more knowledgeable audience. Moreover, report texts are usually organized in sections under subheadings keyed to a table of contents rather than being continuous, like most essays, and they are more likely to contain tables and graphic illustrations.

Report assignments can be of several different kinds. For example, following a field-trip, survey, or interview you may be asked to write an objective account of your findings. Depending on the course and the instructor, you may have to offer your own conclusions.

In business courses, you may have to prepare a report analyzing a business problem or marketing opportunity, putting forward recommendations and perhaps a plan for their implementation. The emphasis is on concise presentation of practical information tightly organized under subheadings. A one-page abstract or "executive summary" precedes the text and provides a brief overview of its content.

Book Report

In some courses, you will read a book and then summarize its content in a book report. Or you may be asked to read several publications—books, articles, reports, etc.—and then outline what the authors said, perhaps evaluating your findings as well.

Summary

In a summary (or précis) you condense the content of an article or excerpt from a longer work into 20-30 percent (or some other prescribed percentage) of its original length. For instance, you may have to summarize a 500-word article in 100 to 150 words. *In your own words*, restate only the thesis, main points, and conclusion. Occasionally you may use a term or phrase that cannot be altered without losing an essential meaning. Omit the author's specific examples and illustrations. A summary is a miniature of the original—briefer and simpler. It presents only the main ideas, from the author's point of view, showing that you clearly understand what you have read. *Write as though you are that author.* You should never say, "The author thinks . . ." or "In my opinion . . ." or anything that indicates you are writing from your own point of view. A summary tests your ability to read with understanding, not to judge.

Critique

In some courses, such as Philosophy, you may be asked to criticize (analyze and evaluate) an author's argument or point of view. Begin by summarizing the passage in your own words, showing the various steps the author has taken in building toward a conclusion. If you agree with the overall statement, try to extend it, using your own examples; if you disagree, give good reasons. Some instructors permit the use of the first-person "I" in critique writing.

*   *   *

Conventions of style vary for different kinds of essays in different disciplines. This manual describes and exemplifies several of the most commonly used styles. When you are given an essay assignment, ask your instructor about which style you should use.

Parts of Essays

Title Page

On a separate, unlined sheet, place the title of the essay in ALL CAPITAL letters, your name and registration number, the course and section, the instructor's name, the name of the college or university, and the date. Imitate the order, arrangement, and spacing of the sample layout on page 9. Leave the back of the title page blank.

Title

The title presents the first words a reader encounters, so it is very important. Make it accurate and specific—and, if possible, catchy. RESEARCH ESSAY is not a title at all; it merely indicates a general kind of essay. THE HUDSON'S BAY COMPANY could be the title of a heavy volume; it has far too much scope for a term paper. THE HUDSON'S BAY COMPANY AS A COLONIAL POWER: 1670-1770 is better, because it makes a clear promise about the essay's contents. An effective title invites the reader to resolve a conflict, explore a mystery, discover a meaning.

For a term paper, a *subtitle* can help by providing additional information, as in the examples below. Note that both title layouts use a colon to precede the subtitle.

COLLATERAL DAMAGE: HOW MILITARY EUPHEMISMS
AFFECT OUR PERCEPTION OF THE GULF WAR

Note: this subtitle provides further details to explain a vague title and clarify the true subject.

UNBORN DRUNKS:
THE TRAGEDY OF FETAL ALCOHOL SYNDROME

Note: here emotional language suggests an appeal to feelings and social awareness.

Perhaps you are writing about a published work and wish to include its title as part of your own. If it is separately published (e.g., a book, film, work of art, play, or television program), underline or italicize that part of your title: ANIMAL SYMBOLISM IN FINDLEY'S THE WARS (book); ALLUSIONS TO CHRISTIAN MYTH IN FIELD OF DREAMS (film); THE TRIUMPH OF WOMEN IN ARTEMISIA GENTILLESCHI'S JUDITH BEHEADING HOLOFERNES (painting).

Sample Title Page

CULTURE CLASH: THE IMPACT OF
EUROPEAN SETTLEMENT ON THE KWAKIUTL

Leslie Peeler
90102385

English 128
Section 1
Dr. M. Smith
Northwest Community College
20 March 1993

If you include the title of a poem, song, short story, essay, magazine or newspaper article, scholarly paper, or any other *part* of a longer work, place it in double quotation marks: POETIC ELEMENTS IN COHEN'S LYRIC FOR "FAMOUS BLUE RAINCOAT" (song); DECODING THE DECEPTION: ARENDT'S "LYING IN POLITICS" (essay).

Avoid a title that is a complete sentence. Instead, use phrases—hints rather than flat statements. Do not place a period after your title (or any other heading or subheading).

Contents

A table of contents is used only for reports or long essays that require several distinct parts identified by subheadings. It should appear on a separate, unnumbered page, following the title page. It lists the subheadings and their accompanying page numbers. Label the page "Contents" centered at the top, and word the list and the subheadings in the text identically. If you need a complex system of subdivisions, consult Turabian.

Epigraph

You may wish to put a touch of polish on your essay (especially on a longer research essay) by attaching an epigraph—a striking, pertinent quotation that helps prepare the reader's mind for the text that immediately follows. Center the epigraph three inches from the top of a separate page. Do not use quotation marks. Place the name of the author below the epigraph flush right, followed by the title of the work. Do not include bibliographical details about the source of the quotation.

Text

A basic essay expounds *one* main thesis—the idea you wish to prove. Readers generally expect to understand clearly from your *beginning* paragraph what this thesis is (sometimes, however, you may build up to your thesis statement, placing it in a dramatic position later in the text). The *middle* of the essay develops the thesis by providing details, reasons, examples, comparisons, contrasts, definitions, research, or other evidence for your main claim. Each paragraph presents *one* aspect of your main idea; it takes one step toward your conclusion in the *ending* paragraph.

Do *not* indicate a new paragraph by leaving an extra line space. Instead, indent the first line of each paragraph *five letter spaces*. Double space the text throughout the essay. (The only exception is a recommendation to single space block quotations—see "Lengthy Quotations," page 24.)

An essay text is usually continuous. Still, as noted above, long essays or reports often require subheadings. These should be in upper and lower case letters, underlined, and centered on the page with an extra line space above.

Illustrations and Tables

A graph, diagram, picture, or table should appear where it most logically fits—preferably right after your first mention of it in the text. Do not include illustrations unless your assignment requires them; and do not include them without introducing them in the text.

If you use several graphs or diagrams, number them with arabic numerals: Fig. 1, Fig. 2, etc. Place this label *below* the illustration, starting at the margin; continue on the same line with a simple legend or caption; then add a short parenthetical reference to indicate the source. Single space the caption if more than one line is needed. Provide a full citation in your list of works cited.

For tables, place the heading "Table" on a line of its own *above* the material; add an arabic numeral if you use more than one table; leave a line space, and center a descriptive caption; include a reference immediately *below* the table; give a citation in your works cited.

Appendix

An appendix appears at the end of the essay, immediately following the text, under the centered heading "Appendix". It may include a graph, table, or other documentary material too extensive to put in the body of the essay without breaking its continuity. Indicate an appendix with a parenthetical note in your text at the place you want the reader to refer to it, e.g., "(see Appendix)". If you use more than one, add arabic numerals to the headings and to the text references, e.g., "(see Appendix 2)".

Content Notes

Regardless of whether you use MLA style, with source references in your text, or the note style of documentation (see pages 62-67 for discussion and examples), you may also wish to include content notes in your essays. They provide further information, comment, or explanation that cannot be accommodated within the text. Use such notes *sparingly*: the information they contain must be of fundamental interest.

For a single note in the entire essay (you are using source references in the text), place a superscript asterisk * (a half space above the line) immediately after the item you wish to comment upon. Write the note (single spaced) after a matching asterisk at the foot of the same page (see page 63 for layout of footnotes).

Here is a sample note:

```
    * As Lewis Mumford says, in Herman Melville, "one
might garner a whole book of verse from Moby-Dick" (181).
W.O. Matthiessen, in American Renaissance (426), goes
further and actually sets out lines in blank verse form.
```

For a second note, use two asterisks ** both in your text and at the bottom of the page.

For more than two notes (a remote possibility in a short essay), use arabic numerals as superscripts after each item. Number them consecutively throughout the text. If you are using the note system of documentation, combine your content notes with your reference notes and number them together. Place the notes at the bottoms of the appropriate pages, or depending on number and length, gather them as endnotes on a separate page immediately following the text.

Works Cited

This is a list of *all* the sources you referred to in your text, including nonprint sources such as audiotapes, records, films, etc. Whenever you use someone else's work in any way, except to confirm common knowledge, you should supply *both* a text reference *and* a corresponding works cited entry. You must also give a reference for material you have paraphrased but not necessarily quoted; again, a citation is required.

Some instructors expect you to subdivide your list of works cited using appropriate subtitles: "Books," "Articles," "Interviews," etc., or "Primary Sources" and "Secondary Sources." Usually, however, you will simply arrange all the citations in a single, undifferentiated list at the end of the essay under the heading "Works Cited." (See pages 39-41 for a description of how to present entries in works cited.)

Presentation of Essays

During your first year or two in college, your instructors will probably accept hand-written essays, but later on they will undoubtedly expect them to be typed. So, if you are unable to type or use a word processor, you should seriously consider learning how (or be prepared to pay for the service). A word of warning, though: don't type your essays until you have developed a reasonable level of proficiency, i.e., don't use your essays for typing practice.

It is not just a matter of turning out well-presented papers. When you acquire adequate keyboard skills, you will be able to speed up the writing process and make it more effective. It is a waste of study time to laboriously type up a text you have already hand written and revised. Instead, you should compose directly onto the machine to produce a cleaner text that is easier to edit. The word processor in particular allows, indeed encourages, the use of a variety of editing techniques—adding and deleting, cutting and pasting, etc.—that will almost certainly help you improve your writing. And the ability to store, retrieve, and print text upon command is a valuable asset.

An electronic typewriter, even with its limited memory, will offer some editing features, and like the word processor will permit you to store text and print hard copies whenever you wish. Even if you use a regular typewriter, you can easily manipulate your text using scissors and Scotch tape, cutting and pasting physically rather than electronically. Typing facilitates editing, as well as producing a better looking text.

Appearance *is* important. A well-presented essay gives the reader confidence that the writer has all aspects of the writing process under control.

Be sure to proofread your text carefully. When typewriting, use correction fluid or a correction tape when making minor text changes. For last-minute corrections, use the proofreader's symbols shown below (your instructor may use them when marking your essay).

1. Use 8½ x 11 inch paper.
2. Do not present an essay written in pencil. Write, or type, on one side of the page only. Leave the other side blank.
3. Double space the lines of text, whether you type, use a word processor, or write by hand.
4. If you use a word processor, be sure your printer is of reasonable quality (avoid the cheaper kinds of dot-matrix printers). Remember to keep a copy of the essay on a back-up disk. Word-processing programs vary—stick as closely as your program will allow to the conventions given in this manual.

5. When using a word processor or electronic typewriter, left justify the text, leaving the right margin "ragged." Make sure the print in your text is sharp and black; it must be easy to read (and photocopy).

6. Use blank paper for typed essays, lined paper for hand-written ones. Use blank paper for diagrams, tables, and title pages.

7. When page numbering, count but *do not put the number* on the first text page (page 2 is thus the first numbered page). Number all subsequent pages consecutively, including pages for appendices, endnotes, and works cited. Either center the number or place it against the right-hand margin, one-half inch from the top of the page. Do not punctuate the number.

8. Either present your essay in a folder with the text on the right-hand pages (in which case, put your name, the course, and the section number on the outside cover), or staple the pages at the top left-hand corner. If in doubt, ask your instructor.

9. If you present your essay in a folder, leave a 1½-inch margin at the left of the page to allow for hole punching. Leave a 1-inch margin elsewhere. If you staple the pages at the top left-hand corner, leave a 1-inch margin all round. See the sample on page 15, and try to achieve a similar effect.

10. If you type or hand write your essay, make a photocopy and keep it safe—it is rare, but not unknown, for instructors to lose students' essays.

Here are some of the most commonly used proofreader's symbols to aid you in the final correcting of your text:

Symbol:	Meaning:
∧	or insert word∧phrase
——	delete word or phrase
——	change correct a word or phrase
stet	restore original text
/	make lower case
#	insert space
‿	close up space
/	separate words
∽	transpose letters words or
¶	begin new paragraph
no ¶	no new paragraph

14

Sample Text Page

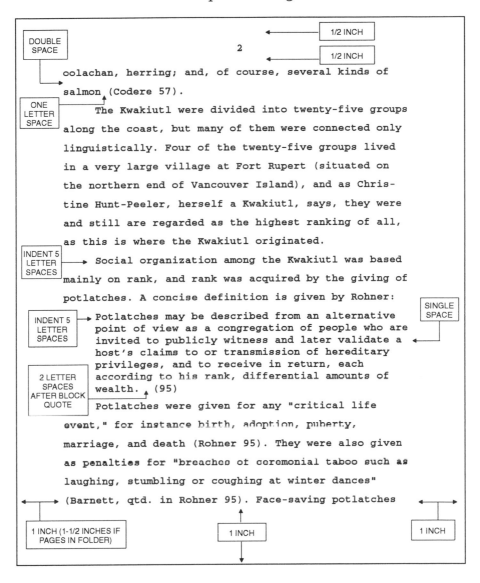

This sample page is a guide for the final draft of an essay employing parenthetical references. It shows the first numbered page (i.e., page 2)—note the position and form of the number. The text is *double* spaced; the block quotation is *single* spaced and indented *five* letter spaces from the left margin. Note the text references and the placement of the parentheses. The Hunt-Peeler reference in the second paragraph is to an interview, so no page number appears.

Handling Mechanical Details

In polishing your final draft, pay close attention to the many mechanical details that need to be checked. For full discussion and exemplification of them, see the *MLA Handbook*. Meanwhile, here are some items that regularly draw criticism when mishandled.

1. Spell out round numbers that can be expressed in one or two words (e.g., eight, twenty-seven, two hundred), and use numerals for the rest (e.g., 8½, 127, 3,420). Spell out a number that begins a sentence. Retain numerals where they occur in names or titles (e.g., 49th Avenue). Use numerals also for dates, times, measurements, and money. Avoid mixing numerals and spelled-out numbers (use all numerals, e.g., 8½ by 11, not 8½ by eleven).

2. The simplest way to write a date is 4 July 1976. Equally acceptable is July 4, 1976. Write 62 BC, but AD 62.

3. In this manual, all essay examples requiring italics use underlining according to the convention that underlining equals italics. However, with the advent of the word processor and the electronic typewriter, italic typefaces are quite widely available. If you have an italic typeface on your machine, use it when required (but do *not* type your entire essay in italic). Otherwise, underline in place of italics (see the next item).

4. Underline, or italicize, the title of a book, magazine, newspaper, film, play, opera, long poem, tape, radio or television program, or record album. Use *quotation marks* to indicate a part within a whole: a chapter, story, article, essay, aria, short poem, or song title. Underline, or italicize, foreign words that are not part of our ordinary speech: underline "Weltschmerz," but not "milieu."

5. Use abbreviations in your notes and works cited entries, but avoid them in your text, except for conventional forms such as "a.m.," "Mr.," "CIA," and "UN." In your text, spell out the names of months and measurements such as "inch," "pound," and "meter." Except in well-known cases (such as NATO), spell out the name of an organization on first use, and place the abbreviation in a parenthesis immediately after—e.g., Los Angeles Police Department (LAPD); thereafter use the abbreviation alone. Punctuate abbreviations with care. Omit periods in capitalized abbreviations, but include periods with lower case abbreviations (see examples above). If in doubt, consult the *MLA Handbook*.

6. Avoid contractions. Write "do not" instead of "don't"; "cannot" instead of "can't," etc. Your tone is thus more formal, a desirable effect in most essays.

7. Misuse of the possessive apostrophe is annoying. None of the personal pronouns needs an apostrophe. The word "it's" means either "it is" or "it has." The proper form of this possessive pronoun is "its."
8. The general rule is to add 's to the singular of *any* possessive noun (the cat's collar, Mr. Jones's house), but an apostrophe alone to the plural if it ends in *s* (the cats' collars, the Joneses' house). Plural nouns that do *not* end in *s* form the possessive by adding 's (children's).
9. The convention for using apostrophes with names ending in *s* is variable. Some writers will call an essay by George Williams "Williams' essay"; others, "Williams's essay." The latter is preferable since the former, read aloud, sounds like "William's essay"—which is wrong. If a possessive form sounds awkward aloud, consider using a prepositional phrase: instead of "Jesus's wisdom," write "the wisdom of Jesus."
10. Learn the basic rules of punctuation thoroughly. Whether it seems fair or not, grammar and punctuation—they are closely related—greatly influence your reader's response to your work. Faulty or irregular punctuation can be confusing, and may lead a reader to underestimate your ideas.
11. Bad spelling is distracting, and an otherwise good essay is likely to be penalized for it. Take responsibility for your spelling errors: develop a list of misspelled words; review that list when you proofread your final draft; buy a good dictionary and consult it whenever you doubt your spelling.

Avoiding Discriminatory Language

Nowadays readers, writers, publishers, and teachers are increasingly sensitive to evidences of bias in written language. As a courtesy to your reader, and as part of your social responsibility as a writer, you should avoid language that discriminates against other people with respect to their gender, race, social class, sexual orientation, and religious beliefs.

The English language contains a built-in bias in favour of males, but the convention that says "a person" is always "he" can easily be overcome. In some cases, the phrase "he or she" may be substituted. Often a switch to the plural will circumvent the problem. You should adopt these and other similar usages including gender neutral nouns (e.g. "worker" instead of "workman," "letter carrier" instead of "mailman") to ensure that, unwittingly, you do not offend your reader by an inappropriate choice of words.

Avoiding Plagiarism

Avoid plagiarism. It is something you consciously or unconsciously "commit" when using the words or ideas of another person as though they were your own—a sort of literary sin.

When, without acknowledgment, you (1) repeat "someone else's sentences, more or less verbatim," (2) use someone else's "particularly apt phrase," (3) paraphrase someone else's idea, or (4) retrace the steps of someone else's line of thought, you have committed plagiarism (Gibaldi and Achtert 22-23). It is "the false assumption of authorship: the wrongful act of taking the product of another person's mind, and presenting it as one's own" (Lindey, qtd. in Gibaldi and Achtert 21).

Note the quotation marks and documentation in the preceding sentences. You, too, *must* acknowledge by means of conventional text references, or appropriate notes, your borrowing of someone else's words, ideas, data, or other information. Penalties for plagiarism can be severe. If you suspect you are plagiarizing, you probably are, as your instructor will easily recognize. Ironically it is easier and more impressive to show off your well-chosen sources than to try to conceal them.

When you find secondary material you want to use in your essay, there are three ways to incorporate it: by *paraphrase, summary*, or *quotation*. Since all three are vital components of several kinds of research papers, and since each is susceptible to plagiarism, they deserve separate consideration.

Read the following excerpt taken from page 2 of the introduction to *A Casebook of Ideologies*, by Macdonald Burbidge:

> A reader should also be aware of the distinction between empirical claims—that is, those which describe what *is, was* or *will be the case*, and which can be tested by observation, experience, and experiment—and moral claims, which are claims about what *ought to be the case*, and which are grounded upon some type of moral principle. For example, one may point out the empirical fact that ordinary people in Chile do not have freedom of speech, since it is empirically observable that if they do speak out, they may be flung in jail. But those who claim that Chileans ought to be free to speak without fear of punishment are making a moral claim, and it therefore makes sense to ask them for the conclusive principle upon which the claim is based. For example, it could be based upon the Christian view that God has willed that humans be free, the utilitarian view that such freedom will in the long run lead to the maximization of happiness, or an *a priori* (self-evident) claim, such as might be made by a follower of Kant, that each person has a moral right to free speech regardless of the law. (Emphasis added.)

Paraphrase

This term signifies the restatement of a short passage in other words.

REASONS TO EMPLOY PARAPHRASES:

1. You are more concerned with the original author's points than with the actual words—substance rather than style.
2. Too much quotation clutters the page; paraphrase provides variety, an alternative way of incorporating a source.
3. Your own expression, or "voice," should dominate the essay.

FORM OF PARAPHRASES:

1. Use mainly short passages of paraphrase (one or two sentences), combining them with quotations and your own comments.
2. Try to parallel the structure, content, and length of the original.
3. It is not acceptable to repeat the original and merely alter or cut a few words; instead, rephrase all the information *in your own words*.
4. Handle a key word, startling phrase, highly technical, or untranslatable term by *quoting* it.
5. Maintain a similar level of diction; the paraphrase should not be a watered-down version of the original.

Note: in special kinds of essays such as book reports and scientific research reports, paraphrase and summary may comprise a major component of the writing. An excellent place to find examples of combined paraphrase, summary, and quotation is in any volume of "Abstracts" in the reference section of the library.

In regular essays, you should paraphrase the more routine statements in the original source, and quote only the most striking, significant portions. They will then stand out against a background of paraphrase. If you quote too much, the impact of individual quotations is weakened. You should therefore differentiate the more important statements (quotations) from the less important (paraphrase).

PARAPHRASE OF THE TWO HIGHLIGHTED SENTENCES ABOVE:

```
A person is making a moral claim when he or she states
that to speak with impunity should be the inalienable
right of all people. Such a claim might be rooted in the
spiritual belief that free speech is a right bestowed by a
Higher Power; in the pragmatic belief that this liberty is
useful and necessary in order to achieve ultimate
satisfaction in life; or in the Kantian belief that,
beyond the bounds of any instituted authority, free speech
```

is the inherent right of every human being--an a priori
truth (Burbidge 2).

This is an acceptable paraphrase. It restates all of the principal ideas of the passage, maintaining the basic order, integrity, and force of the original while recasting it in a fresh way.

A parenthetical reference *must* be included here to acknowledge the secondary source of the paraphrased ideas. By turning to the works cited page, the reader will find this citation:

Burbidge, Macdonald. A Casebook of Ideologies:
    Liberalism, Communism, Meritocracy, Conservatism,
    Democratic Socialism, Anarchism. Vancouver, BC:
    Vancouver Community College Press, 1990.

With this information, the reader could then go to the library and find the book, turn to page 2, and read more. Without this reference and corresponding citation, the author of the above paraphrase is guilty of plagiarism: the ideas have been "borrowed" without acknowledgment.

Summary

A summary is a condensation of a much longer passage. A whole book could be summarized in a sentence; a chapter, in a paragraph. It all depends on how much detail you wish to retain. The entire original selection above might be summarized as follows:

Empirical and moral claims differ significantly: whereas
the former rely solely upon perception and scientific
measurement to describe objective reality, the latter rely
on idealisms or felt certainties about what reality should
or might be. Under an oppressive regime, freedom of speech
is forbidden to most people, as the empiricist observes;
the moralist, on the other hand, witnesses the often
severe violation of fundamental human rights and makes
judgments based on deep religious, pragmatic, or a priori
principles.

As written, this is plagiarism. The *whole pattern of thought* has been lifted from its author without notice. The passage would become acceptable, and also more interesting and credible, if the source were credited. Here is one way of introducing the source into the text of the essay:

```
As Burbidge points out, empirical and moral claims differ
significantly: . . . deep religious, pragmatic, or a
priori principles (2).
```

Introducing the author at the beginning and concluding with the page reference is a simple way to frame a paraphrase or summary, distinguishing it from the rest of the text. You have the option of placing the author's name in the sentence, as shown here, or in the parenthetical reference that usually comes at the end of every summary or paraphrase. See pages 31-38 for explanation of the content and placement of references to sources.

Quotation

The term *quotation* refers to your use of the *actual words* of another person, whether from a printed text, a radio interview, a lecture, etc. You must distinguish his or her words from your own by using quotation marks or other conventions (described below in "Quoting Effectively"). Quotation without acknowledgment, however, still produces plagiarism, as in the following example:

```
The moral issue of free speech is particularly important
today, especially in countries where people are flung in
jail or even killed just for speaking out against the
regime. There are different reasons free speech is morally
right and ought to be the case, based on conclusive
principles. The Christian idea is that God wants us to be
free; a utilitarian thinker believes that happiness will
be maximized; others believe the self-evident idea of
Kant, that everyone has "a moral right to freedom of
speech" no matter what the law says.
```

This is a mishmash of plagiarisms. The writer has copied the pattern of thinking of the original, used quotation without employing quotation marks, misquoted a phrase, and paraphrased extensively—all without crediting the source. The quotation marks hint at the writer's good intentions, but half measures are not enough. To make matters worse, Kant has been misrepresented.

In contrast, the presence of summary statements, paraphrases, and quotations—with appropriate documentation—will lend credibility and the force of authority to the main points of your research essay.

Often individual sentences will contain three kinds of language: your own words (introducing the topic, drawing conclusions, etc.), paraphrase or sum-

21

mary (source material expressed in your words), and direct quotation (word for word from the original). These three make a powerful combination.

Quoting Effectively

Often our reading inspires us to respond in writing; our ideas and expression are profoundly stimulated, guided, and even formed by the words of others. To invite the thought and language of other writers into our own work affirms our participation with other minds in the ceaseless effort to make sense of things. Our writing becomes more interesting and complex.

Purpose

In many courses, especially in the humanities and social sciences, the instructor expects your essays to reflect your reading. Quotations from respected authors in the discipline can enliven almost any kind of essay by introducing another voice or point of view, illustrating major points, and reinforcing your arguments. Find the strongest quotations you can—surprising details, vivid statements of controversy, prime examples, insightful phrases and sentences that seem to condense a large idea into a memorable truth.

Note: since you have to provide references and corresponding citations for *all* quotations, it is essential that you make notes painstakingly when doing library research: use quotation marks to distinguish quotations from paraphrase or summary; record page numbers for each quotation; use ellipsis periods (see page 25) to indicate omissions.

How Much Quotation?

Avoid very long quotations, especially in a short essay. Quote only key passages. Make sure you know the desired balance between quotation and text. In English essays, usually 10-15 percent of the text is quotation, but a research essay or book report may require more. Ask your instructor. Excessive quotation suggests you are not doing enough of your own thinking; too little indicates you have not done the research.

References for Quotations

If a word, phrase, or sentence deserves to be quoted, it also requires a reference. Unless otherwise instructed, give a reference for *all* quotations, even brief ones. Typically, a reference includes an author's name and a page number. The name may appear in your sentence or in a parenthesis; the page number *always* appears in a parenthesis. (See "Sample References," pages 34-37). When several quotations in a row are taken from the same page, a single parenthesis after the last quotation of a series refers to all the quotations following the preceding reference.

Brief Quotations

Incorporate brief quotations—key words, phrases, or sentences—as smoothly as possible *within* your own sentences. Place quotation marks around them:

```
Lawrence called the novel the "one bright book of life"
(126), elevating it above all other forms of literature.
```

Note: the quotation is a natural grammatical element of this sentence, needing only the quotation marks and the reference. Avoid using phrases such as "In the following quotation" or "as shown in this quote" since the quotation marks already indicate you are quoting.

A quotation can appear at the beginning, middle, or end of your sentence. Try to provide variety:

```
"The horror! The horror!"--this is Kurtz's last judgment
(608).
```

```
Atwood opposes any theory that limits expression: "Theory
is a positive force when it vitalizes and enables, but a
negative one when it is used to amputate and repress, to
create a batch of self-righteous rules and regulations"
(24).
```

Note: use a colon after a *complete* statement that introduces a quotation.

After phrases such as "she says," "he writes," "the report claimed," "the character responds," "the author maintains," "the law states," etc., which are not complete statements, use a comma to introduce the following quotation:

```
Malcolm X, the author suggests, "brought about a more
aggressive popular language that helped to fire up a
generation of poets" (Davis).
```

Omit this comma if you replace it with the word "that." For example, She concludes, "We are free . . ." but She concludes that "We are free . . ."

Note: the parenthetical reference to Davis, above, refers to a one-page newspaper article, making a page number unnecessary since it appears in works cited.

You may subordinate a quotation by placing it in a parenthesis. The page number is in *square brackets* to show a parenthesis within a parenthesis:

```
Ruskin answers the initial questions ("How does one define
children's literature?" and "How has the language of
children's literature changed?" [214]) with a good deal of
humor.
```

Use a pair of dashes, instead of parentheses or commas, as a way of emphasizing whatever is between them, including quoted material:

```
Ruskin is firm in her stand that many fairy tales,
nonsense poems, and folk legends--"originally intended for
an audience of any age at all" (215)--prove there is
continuity between childhood and adulthood.
```

Lengthy Quotations

Quotations that would comprise *four or more* lines of prose on your page should be set off from your text in *block* form. (See page 29 for how to quote poetry.) Leave a line space (some instructors prefer two) before and after the quotation; indent the whole quotation *five* letter spaces from the left margin; *single space* the quotation itself. Do not use quotation marks in a block quotation unless they appear in the original—to indicate dialogue, for example. Like other quotations, the block quotation must be a logical, grammatical part of your sentence. Usually it is introduced by a colon following a complete statement:

```
While this movement in art was a rebellion against morbid,
academic values, Ernst Fischer is critical of it, insofar
as it enacts and confirms individualism at the expense of
social change:

     Impressionism, dissolving the world of light,
     breaking it up into colors, recording it as a
     sequence of sensory perceptions, became more and
     more expressive of a very complex, very short-term
     subject-object relationship. The individual, reduced
     to loneliness, concentrating upon himself,
     experiences the world as a set of nerve stimuli,
     impressions, and moods, as a "shimmering chaos," as
     "my" experience, "my" sensation.  (71)

In a world that is increasingly fragmented and
dehumanized, the role of art as a force for achieving
political awareness . . .
```

The example shows a complete statement, followed by a colon, introducing a block quotation. Quotation marks appear only because they occur in Fischer's text. An additional indenting of *three* letter spaces indicates Fischer's paragraphing. In block quotations only, *two* letter spaces precede the page reference, which is unpunctuated.

You may find a quotation that is shorter than four lines and wish to present it in block form in order to give it extraordinary emphasis. Do this rarely, but if you must, its content should be worth all the attention it is receiving.

The *MLA Handbook* recommends an alternative layout for block quotations: after *one* line space, begin a new line, indent *ten* spaces from the left margin, and *double* space the quotation. This method may be convenient for use with some word-processing programs. Single spacing, however, as shown above, sets off the quotation more in keeping with the design of printed books. If in doubt, ask your instructor which method you should use.

Common Faults

Do not sprinkle your text with quotations arbitrarily. Do not try to make a quotation serve as the grammatical subject of a sentence (e.g., `"Art will disappear as life gains more equilibrium" proves what Mondrian means`). Do not insert space after opening or before closing quotation marks. Do not let a quotation stand on its own as an independent sentence; instead, introduce it with your own comment, perhaps mentioning the author's name. In every case, your own sentence must in some way surround the quotation, making it a coherent, natural part of your text. (Test whether or not a quotation fits by reading your whole sentence aloud, including the quotation.) Use quotations to back up your *main* points; do not quote unimportant matters of fact. A quotation should always *add to* the logical development of your discussion, not merely repeat it in different words.

Ellipsis

The ellipsis consists of three spaced periods . . . that indicate the omission of one or more words from a quotation. Do *not* put an ellipsis at the beginnings or ends of short quotations (single words or brief phrases), since they are self-evidently incomplete:

```
The book sets out to define "dehumanization" and what
Marcuse repeatedly calls the "one-dimensional man" (16).
```

Always use an ellipsis when you omit a word or words from *within* a quotation:

```
Lawrence states, "Freud is the starting point . . . in any
study of the mind" (78).
```

Use an ellipsis *to end* a quoted fragment of reasonable length that occurs at the end of your sentence. In such a case, the order of items is: beginning quotation marks, quotation, ellipsis, ending quotation marks, parenthetical reference, and final period:

```
Lawrence goes on to say, "Indeed, we find in Freud our
first true pioneer of the unconscious . . ." (80).
```

Leave a letter space between the last word of the quotation and the first period of the ellipsis.

Use an ellipsis *to introduce a block quotation* that does not begin with a sentence capital. An ellipsis is also necessary at the end of a block quotation which does not end with a period in the original; in this case, use four periods as shown here, with the reference set apart after two letter spaces:

```
In their introduction, Cunningham and Reich encourage us

to slow down, to become contemplative as we approach

artistic and literary works, because it would

        . . . help all of us to savor once again the power
        of language and image. That would be a great boon
        for ordinary life. It would enrich us, and . . .
        help us to be warily skeptical of the almost
        universal abuse of language and the shallowness of
        much of our artificial environment. . . .  (3)
```

When you omit one or more sentences from *within* a quotation, use an ellipsis. *A complete sentence* of quotation must precede and follow the ellipsis, however. After the sentence period, place three spaced periods, leave another space, and continue with the balance of the quotation:

```
Thouless maintains that "We are allowing our brains to

degenerate into mere mechanisms when they were meant for

plasticity and change. . . . Inflexibility of mind would

lead to the extermination of the human race" (129).
```

Do *not*, however, use the three spaced periods to stitch together statements from widely separated areas of the text. The effect is quite misleading. Use your own words to link them.

Brackets

Use square brackets when you must alter, or add, a word or phrase within a quotation to make the quotation fit grammatically, or to supply a proper name to a pronoun lacking a clear antecedent:

```
The same critic writes, "When we first meet him [Hamlet],
a spirit of gloom prevails . . ." (41).
```

Use this device *only when you have to*. Almost any sentence can be rewritten to incorporate the quotation as it originally appears, or the quotation can be trimmed to eliminate the offending word or phrase:

```
The same critic writes that when the audience first
encounters Hamlet, "a spirit of gloom prevails" (41).
```

Errors in Quotations

Occasionally you may come across a serious factual or style error, or a spelling mistake, in a quotation you plan to use. If you wish to draw attention to the error, place the Latin word "sic" (meaning "thus") in square brackets after it, as in the following example:

```
According to J. N. Sullivan, "At the time of writing Moby
Dick [sic] the problem that was to haunt Melville was, as
it were, fairly straightforward" (15).
```

The reader will thus understand that the errors in the title *Moby-Dick* (the lack of italics and a hyphen) occurred in the original source.

Quotation Within a Quotation

In block quotations, preserve quotation marks exactly as they appear in the original—do not supply marks of your own. But when you incorporate a short quotation into your sentence, and any part of that quotation contains double quotation marks, change them to *single* ones.

Original: Hopkins's invention of what he called "sprung rhythm," "instress," and "inscape" provided a sense of liberation to early twentieth-century poets.

Your sentence: ```Ezra Pound is one of many poets who found
"a sense of liberation" in "Hopkins's invention of what he
called 'sprung rhythm,' 'instress,' and 'inscape'" (Markham
61).```

Note: generally, your quotation marks take precedence over the original ones. In the above example, you are quoting both Markham and Hopkins, and so you need both single and double marks to distinguish the original authors. But if you wanted to quote only Hopkins's term(s) and include nothing from Markham, it would *not* be necessary to use more than your own quotation marks.

Incorrect: `Hopkins called this new concept "'instress'"` `because . . .`

Correct: `Hopkins called this new concept "instress"` `because . . .`

Stated as a rule: when you are quoting any one speaker or author, use regular quotation marks. Do not use single quotation marks unless a second speaker intervenes. Note, too, that quotation marks appear around each individual word and phrase in the series quoted above. They are not lumped together as "sprung rhythm, instress, and inscape" because they do not appear together that way in the original source.

Punctuating the Close of Quotations

All punctuation that appears immediately before your closing quotation marks must be grammatical. Thus you do not always have to quote the writer's punctuation, but instead may sometimes supply your own. Your period or comma should go *inside* the quotation marks, unless a parenthetical reference is necessary, in which case your punctuation follows the parenthesis. You should retain the author's question mark or exclamation mark, but not the author's colon, semicolon, or dash when it appears at the end of a quotation.

Original: . . . they are wise and aware; they enjoy life with gusto, yet face and accept death; they not only work productively but creatively, and they obviously love their fellow human beings . . .

Your sentence: `The author admires people who are "wise and` `aware," who "enjoy life with gusto," and who "accept death";` `to him truly sane people function "productively" and "cre-` `atively"; most importantly, they "love their fellow human` `beings" (Peck 125).`

Original: Are we to consider individuals healthy simply because they are not in pain—no matter how much havoc and harm they bring to their fellow human beings?

Your sentence: `Peck asks, "Are we to consider individuals` `healthy . . . no matter how much havoc and harm they bring to` `their fellow human beings?" (125).`

Your sentence: `Can we trust Peck's analysis of "how much harm` `they [evil people] bring to their fellow human beings" (125)?`

28

Note: your punctuation takes precedence over the original. In the second example, your question mark rules the sentence, not Peck's.

Quoting Poetry

Incorporate a line or part of a line of poetry as though you were quoting prose. For example, **Williams's poem is about "how to perform a funeral."** Page and line references are unnecessary when you quote from short poems. Simply acknowledge your source in a content note (see page 11).

For a quotation of two or three lines, indicate line endings with a slash:

```
From the start, Williams's poem is didactic, promising

some kind of ethical lesson: "I will teach you my

townspeople / how to perform a funeral."
```

Leave a letter space before and after the slash. Note that there is *no slash at the beginning or end* of the quotation. To indicate a stanza break, use a pair of slashes // without an extra space between them.

When you quote more than three lines, use *block* form, centered on the page:

```
One passage in particular demonstrates his individual
sense of rhythm:
```

```
            To you
                I can risk words about this

        Mastering them you know
                they are dull
                        servants
        Who say less
                and worse
                        than we feel
```

In a block quotation from a poem, try to duplicate the layout of the original as closely as possible, imitating the poet's margins, spacing, punctuation, and any peculiarities of typography.

Long lines of poetry require special treatment in block form. Indent the first line five letter spaces and run it to the right margin; indent the overflow on your next line(s) three additional letter spaces. What you have shown to be two or more lines will thus be understood as a single line in the original.

Use of Single Quotation Marks

As well as showing a quotation within a quotation, single quotation marks can indicate your ironic use of someone else's term. You may use such marks (sparingly) to stand for a phrase like "so-called": The shelves were stocked with 'natural' food products.

Use of Italics in Quotations

Any word, phrase, or complete sentence that appears in italics in the original source must be italicized or underlined in your quotation.

Original: To start at the end first, *the peak-experience is only good and desirable, and is never experienced as evil or undesirable.*

Your sentence: Maslow begins by claiming that "peak-experience is only good and desirable" (76).

If you wish to emphasize a word or phrase in a quotation, you may italicize or supply underlining, but only if you include a special phrase in acknowledgment:

Daily life, to Lawrence, is merely a facade; the true life is actually to be found in the "subterranean regions of the soul" and in the "primitive" conscious life of the body (94, emphasis added).

Quoting Drama

For brief drama quotations, treat prose dialogue as if it were from a short story or novel, and introduce the name of the character in your sentence. In block quotations of dialogue, indent five letter spaces as usual, but begin with the speaker's name, followed by a colon, and omit any stage directions unless pertinent:

is characterized by constant tension and bickering:
    Charley: Don't get insulted.
    Willy: Don't insult me.
    Charley: I don't see no sense in it. . . . (43)

For verse drama, follow the convention for references described in "References to Literary Works," page 37.

References to Sources in English Essays

Whenever you quote other people's actual words, paraphrase their ideas, or make use of their data or original information, you must acknowledge your indebtedness—both in your text, by using references, and in a list of works cited. Together these two forms of documentation are sufficient for your readers to appreciate the variety and quality of your sources, and to locate them for the purposes of their own research.

Purpose of References

Provide text references (see below for examples) either *within your sentences*, or *in parentheses*, or in combination—

1. to indicate the source, including page number(s) for printed materials, of any quotation you include in your text;
2. to acknowledge your indebtedness for factual information and for ideas paraphrased, or summarized (i.e. not directly quoted), from any source;
3. and to direct readers to the list of works cited for complete details of publication.

Content of References to Printed Sources

A text reference to a printed source *must* contain the following:

1. the last name of the author (or editor, translator, etc.)—*either* in your sentence, *or* as the first item in a parenthesis that follows any quotation, paraphrase, or summary you used;
2. the title of the work, *either* in your sentence, *or* in a parenthesis—*if* you have referred to *more than one work* by the same author;
3. the page number(s) *in a parenthesis* for any quotation, paraphrase, or summary you used.

The content of a parenthetical reference usually takes one of the three following forms:

(87)	—page number alone, when you have already identified the work in your text
(Breit 87)	—author's last name (no punctuation following) and page number

```
(Breit, Writer 87)
```
—author's last name, comma, title (abbreviated from The Writer Observed, a book, hence underlined or italicized) and page number

With few exceptions (the Bible, an encyclopedia, a dictionary, or a one-page article), every parenthetical reference to a printed source will contain a page number. Do not mention page numbers elsewhere in your sentences. For anonymous works, the title (usually abbreviated) replaces the author's name in the parenthesis.

Remember, the parenthesis should *not* repeat details already given in your sentence.

References in Sentences or in Parentheses?

You have a choice: include references either in the body of your sentences or in parentheses. This flexibility allows you to achieve different effects.

1. Einstein and Infeld introduce their history of modern physics as though they were fiction writers: "In imagination there exists the perfect mystery story" (Evolution 3).

This sentence emphasizes the *authors* rather than the source. The inclusion of the abbreviated title in the parenthesis indicates that more than one work by these authors has been referred to, and reveals the specific source of the quotation.

2. In The Evolution of Physics, a layman's guide to physics from Galileo to quantum mechanics and relativity theory, Einstein and Infeld distinguish between Arthur Conan Doyle's and their own "detective novel" (4).

This sentence draws attention to the *text*, as well as mentioning the authors, suggesting that the book itself is central to the discussion.

3. Few would argue with the theory that "Human thought creates an ever-changing picture of the universe" (Einstein and Infeld 9).

Here the sentence is more concerned with the *idea* than with the source; thus the authors are subordinated in the parenthesis.

4. Some modern physicists (e.g., Einstein and Infeld)
   approach their discipline as though it were a creative art
   or a special branch of philosophy.

Since Einstein and Infeld are just two among many, their names are
subordinated, and because nothing has been quoted or paraphrased, there
is no page reference.

The point is that the content of your reference may vary according to what
element you wish to stress in the sentence.

Placement of Parentheses

In the majority of cases, it is appropriate to place the parenthesis at the end
of the sentence in which the reference (paraphrase, summary, or quotation)
occurs. It goes *inside* your period but *outside* any ending quotation marks, as
in the examples below:

Like most authorities, Zinsser emphasizes that unity is
one of the bases of effective writing (46).

According to Zinsser, unity satisfies the reader's
"subconscious need for order" (46).

Sometimes, however, you may end the reference part way through the
sentence and then introduce a new reference or a comment of your own. In
such cases, you should place the parenthesis inside the punctuation at the end
of the clause in which the reference appears:

Unity is one of the bases of effective writing (Zinsser
46); it is not, however, easy to achieve.

If you refer to an author in passing, then place the parenthesis immediately
after his or her name, again inside any adjacent punctuation:

Most authorities, including Zinsser (46) and Strunk and
White (6), emphasize that unity is one of the bases of
effective writing.

When you use a block quotation, place the parenthesis *two* letter spaces
after the final period:

> You learn to write by writing. It is a truism
> worn thin by repetition, but it is still true,
> and it can't be repeated often enough. The only
> way to learn to write is to force yourself to
> produce a certain number of words on a regular
> basis. (Zinsser 45)

The question often arises of what to do with several references occurring in quick succession. Must every clause or sentence contain a parenthesis? Not necessarily. By pulling together research material from the same page of a particular source, you can reference a whole paragraph of text using an author's name, accompanied by a page number in parentheses, in a sentence at the beginning of the paragraph and another page number in parentheses at the end. The reader understands that all the intervening material appears on the page referred to.

Of course, if you refer to material from several different pages, then you must introduce the various page numbers in parentheses. And if you have referred to several different authorities, their names must appear appropriately, too. But often, as suggested above, you will be able to economize on the number of parentheses you use.

Sample References

¶ **AUTHOR'S NAME AND TITLE IN TEXT**
(you referred to entire work so no page number, no parenthesis)

William Zinsser's <u>On Writing Well</u> provides a wealth of good advice about writing.

¶ **AUTHOR'S NAME IN TEXT WITH PAGE NUMBER IN PARENTHESIS** (you did not refer to another work by same author)

As William Zinsser has said, "Unity is the anchor of good writing" (46).

Note: for a *first reference in your sentence*, you should use an author's full name as given on the title page, e.g., William Zinsser. Subsequently, the last name alone will suffice, i.e., Zinsser.

¶ **AUTHOR'S NAME IN TEXT WITH ABBREVIATED TITLE IN PARENTHESIS** (you referred to another work by same author)

As Zinsser has said, "Unity is the anchor of good writing" (<u>Writing</u> 46).

¶ **AUTHOR'S NAME NOT IN TEXT** (so last name in parenthesis)

The beginning writer should always be aware that "Unity is the anchor of good writing" (Zinsser 46).

¶ **AUTHOR'S NAME AND ABBREVIATED TITLE IN PARENTHESIS**
(you referred to another work by the same author)

```
The beginning writer should always be aware that "Unity is
the anchor of good writing" (Zinsser, Writing 46).
```

¶ **TWO OR THREE AUTHORS CITED IN PARENTHESIS**

```
The purely visual impact of writing deserves attention:
"paragraphing calls for a good eye as well as a logical
mind" (Strunk and White 12).
```

¶ **MORE THAN THREE AUTHORS CITED IN TEXT**

```
Lauer et al. discuss ten points that are important in the
writing process (2-3).
```

Note: "et al." is an abbreviation for the Latin *et alii*, meaning "and others."

¶ **MORE THAN THREE AUTHORS CITED IN PARENTHESIS**

```
At least ten points are important in the writing process
(Lauer et al. 2-3).
```

¶ **REFERENCE TO AN INDIRECT SOURCE**
(original author mentioned in text)

```
According to R. D. Laing, "true sanity" requires "the
dissolution of the normal ego, that false self competently
adjusted to our alienated social reality . . ." (qtd. in
Roszak 50).
```

Note: you discovered the quotation from Laing in a work by Roszak, and you wish to use part of it. As shown here, you must acknowledge both authors. The phrase "qtd. in"—the abbreviation for "quoted in"—indicates that your reader can locate the complete Laing quotation by looking under "Roszak" in your works cited. Do not provide an entry under "Laing" unless he is your direct source elsewhere in the essay. If, however, you think the original source may be of special interest to your reader, document it in a content note (see page 11). If you had paraphrased Laing's idea instead of quoting him, the parenthesis would still contain "qtd. in."

¶ REFERENCE TO AN INDIRECT SOURCE

(original author not mentioned in text so included in parenthesis)

```
We are told that "true sanity" requires "the dissolution
of the normal ego, that false self competently adjusted to
our alienated social reality . . ." (Laing, qtd. in Roszak
50).
```

¶ REFERENCE TO AN UNSIGNED ARTICLE

```
In the southern part of the Selkirk Mountains lie "vast
areas of both igneous rocks of Mesozoic age and very
complex metamorphics" ("Selkirk").
```

Note: whenever your source does not provide the author's name, use an abbreviated version of the title. Here "Selkirk" corresponds to the word under which the work is alphabetized in works cited. No page number appears because the article is alphabetized in an encyclopedia, making the reference easily traceable. If the article appears in a periodical or newspaper, provide a page number.

¶ REPEATED REFERENCE TO ONE OR TWO WORKS

When you quote and/or paraphrase from *one* source (a novel, essay, etc.), give a *full footnote for the first reference* (see "The Note Style of Documentation" beginning on page 62), but *use an asterisk* * instead of a number, both in your text and in the footnote. Add to this footnote a short sentence directing the reader to the text references:

```
    * F. Scott Fitzgerald, The Great Gatsby (New York:
Scribner's, 1925) 23. Subsequent page references are also
to this edition.
```

Thus your text will contain references showing page numbers only, as in the following example. No works cited page is necessary since all of the information your reader needs is present in the footnote.

```
Although Nick sees that Tom and Daisy are responsible for
much of Gatsby's tragedy, he seems unable to censure them
completely, realizing that "what he [Tom] had done was, to
him, entirely justified . . ." (180).
```

If you repeatedly refer to only *two* sources, use two asterisks ** in the text for the second one, and a full footnote also headed by two asterisks. This situation often arises in essays that compare or contrast. Your reader must, however, know clearly from your text which source you are referring to; therefore, to avoid confusion, include an author's name or title in your sentence, or in your parenthesis.

If you use more than two sources, follow the regular conventions for text references, and provide a list of works cited.

References to Literary Works

For some literary works, additional details may be required in the reference. For works of classic prose literature available in different editions, you should provide a chapter number, and a book number when relevant, in addition to the page number. Give the page number first; then, after a semi-colon, give the extra detail(s) using abbreviations ("bk." for "book," "ch." for "chapter"):

```
In Tom Jones, Fielding humorously defends his right to
ransack the works of ancient authors without either
acknowledgment or scruple (474-75; bk. 12, ch. 1).
```

Use arabic numerals instead of roman. In the above example, "XII" in the edition cited has been converted into "12." Note, too, that a comma goes between the book and chapter references.

For classic poems and verse plays, you should omit page numbers; instead, provide division numbers—i.e., the number of any book, canto, part, act, or scene—together with the line numbers:

```
                    Give me that man
        That is not passion's slave, and I will wear him
        In my heart's core, ay, in my heart of heart,
        As I do thee.   (Ham. 3.2. 67-70)
```

Note: in a parenthesis, though *not in the text*, the titles of famous works may be abbreviated: thus "Hamlet" becomes "Ham." In an essay exclusively on this play, however, where the source of the quotation is clear, it is not necessary to include the title in the parenthesis. Use periods to separate the numbers: in the above block quotation, "3" is the act number; "2" is the scene number; and "67-70" are the line numbers. Use arabic numerals. Do not signify lines by using the letters "l" or "ll."

References to The Bible or Other Sacred Texts

Unless you indicate otherwise, your reader will assume you are using the King James Version of the Bible, or the standard versions of other sacred works—

```
Few know that after the resurrection Jesus stayed with his
disciples for forty days, "speaking of the things
pertaining to the kingdom of God" (Acts 1:3).
```

Underlining (or italics), page numbers, and works cited entry are unnecessary.

References to the United States Constitution

An entry in works cited is not required for citations of the Constitution. A parenthetical text reference alone will suffice. Use roman numerals for articles and amendments, and arabic numerals for sections. For example:

```
(Constitution, art. V, sec. 2)

(US Constitution, amend XIV, sec. 3)
```

References to Nonprint Sources

When you acknowledge a nonprint source by a reference in your sentence, you eliminate the need for a parenthesis, since no page number is involved. You may include both a name (of a writer, film director, radio or television artist, musician, etc.) and a title (of a play, film, radio or television program, record, audiotape, etc.), as in the following:

```
In Citizen Kane, Orson Welles created a virtual encyclopedia
of film technique.
```

Note: since the emphasis is on the director, his name should precede the title of the film in the list of works cited (see page 53).

Of course, parentheses will often still be required, especially for the acknowledgment of facts, information, and ideas from a source not integral to your discussion:

```
Bizarre Books, soon to be published by Macmillan, is a
bizarre book listing and describing some of the bizarrest
works ever to appear on a hopeful bookseller's shelves (As
It Happens).
```

Note: there is no reason here to introduce the source of the item (a radio program) in the sentence, so it is placed in the parenthesis.

Works Cited

The works cited page should list *every* source you actually used in your text and for which you provided a text reference (do not fabricate a list of vaguely pertinent works you did not directly refer to). In the text-referencing system, this list is the sole provider of publishing (or broadcasting) details.

For book details, refer to the title page and the copyright page (the reverse of the title page), *not the cover*. Make a note of the title in full (including subtitle), the author(s), the city of publication, and the page number(s) for each reference. Other details should be recorded if present: editor(s); translator; author of foreword, afterword, preface, or introduction (only if named on the title page); edition and volume numbers; article, essay, story, and poem titles from collections; and whatever else may be necessary to enable your reader to track down the source you used. Save unnecessary trips to the library by writing down *full* citations as you do your research.

Record equivalent details for nonprint sources. Refer to record sleeves, cassette labels, introductory radio announcements, film and television credits, etc.

Remember that only some of these details go into your text references, while others are reserved for works cited.

Follow these rules when you prepare your list:

1. Center the words "Works Cited" half an inch below the page number. The list always appears as the last page(s) of the essay. Number each page, continuing the numbering of the text.
2. For *every* source mentioned in your text, provide a corresponding entry in your works cited. The text reference and the entry in works cited must match.
3. Do not subdivide the list into categories unless asked to by your instructor.
4. Begin the first line of each entry at the left margin; indent subsequent lines of that entry by *five* letter spaces.
5. Double space each entry, and double space between entries.
6. Do *not* number the entries.
7. List entries *alphabetically* by the *last name* of the first author (or director, commentator, creative artist, etc.) mentioned in the work's publishing or broadcasting information.
8. When no author is given, alphabetize the entry by the first word in the title. Disregard "A," "An," or "The," but leave the article in its usual order.

Sample Works Cited Page

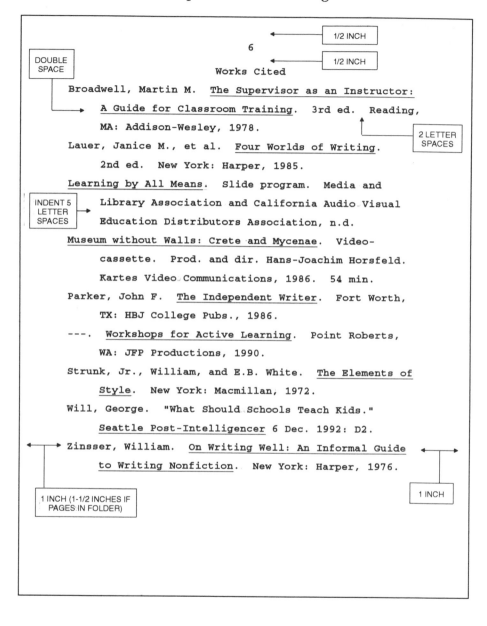

DOUBLE SPACE

1/2 INCH

1/2 INCH

6

Works Cited

Broadwell, Martin M. The Supervisor as an Instructor:
A Guide for Classroom Training. 3rd ed. Reading,
MA: Addison-Wesley, 1978.

2 LETTER SPACES

Lauer, Janice M., et al. Four Worlds of Writing.
2nd ed. New York: Harper, 1985.

Learning by All Means. Slide program. Media and

INDENT 5 LETTER SPACES

Library Association and California Audio Visual
Education Distributors Association, n.d.

Museum without Walls: Crete and Mycenae. Video-
cassette. Prod. and dir. Hans-Joachim Horsfeld.
Kartes Video Communications, 1986. 54 min.

Parker, John F. The Independent Writer. Fort Worth,
TX: HBJ College Pubs., 1986.

---. Workshops for Active Learning. Point Roberts,
WA: JFP Productions, 1990.

Strunk, Jr., William, and E.B. White. The Elements of
Style. New York: Macmillan, 1972.

Will, George. "What Should Schools Teach Kids."
Seattle Post-Intelligencer 6 Dec. 1992: D2.

Zinsser, William. On Writing Well: An Informal Guide
to Writing Nonfiction. New York: Harper, 1976.

1 INCH (1-1/2 INCHES IF PAGES IN FOLDER)

1 INCH

40

9. Capitalize the first and last words in the title (and subtitle, if any), and all the principal words. Do *not* capitalize articles, prepositions, coordinating conjunctions, or the "to" in infinitives. Separate a title and a subtitle with a colon.

10. Underline (or italicize) the title (and subtitle) of a separately published work; put quotation marks around article and essay titles.

11. Give the first city of publication listed on the title page or copyright page. To the name of an unfamiliar city, add an identifying detail: the abbreviated name of a US state, Canadian province, or English county, etc.

12. Give the commonly used *short* form of a publisher's name, omitting Company, Inc., etc. Use "Harper," but not "Harper and Row Inc."

13. For books, give the year of publication recorded on the title page or on the copyright page after the symbol © (but do *not* include this symbol). Give the last *edition* date, but ignore reprint dates. If no date is given, write "n.d."

14. For daily and weekly publications, give the full date (day, month, year) of issue; for monthly publications give the month and year.

15. For motion pictures, records, tapes, and other media, give the year of release or issue. Give the full date for radio and television broadcasts, and interviews.

16. For most nonprint sources, name the medium immediately after the title. See page 53 for further details and examples.

17. Do *not* give page numbers unless you are citing an article in a journal, periodical, or newspaper, or an item in a collection (such as a short story or poem, etc.). Then give the page numbers of the *whole* article or item.

18. *Punctuate each entry carefully.* The model works cited page (page 40) and the sample entries that follow indicate the conventions for punctuating citations. Use a period followed by *two* letter spaces after each major division in a citation. Use a comma between an author's last and first names, and between the publisher's name and the year of publication, but use a colon after the city of publication.

Sample Citations

The list of works cited should employ the same conventions of indentation, order of items, use of underlining or quotation marks, punctuation, abbreviation, etc., illustrated below and in the sample page. Most of the types of sources you are likely to use are exemplified. *To cite a source, find a corresponding example from the entries that follow, and imitate the style.* If you can find no suitable model, consult the *MLA Handbook* (pages 86-154).

Print Sources

¶ BOOK WITH ONE AUTHOR

```
Zinsser, William.  On Writing Well: An Informal Guide to
    Writing Nonfiction.  New York: Harper, 1976.
```

Note: leave *two letter spaces* after each major section of your citation, as shown throughout these examples.

¶ BOOK WITH TWO OR THREE AUTHORS

```
Strunk, Jr., William, and E. B. White.  The Elements of
    Style.  New York: Macmillan, 1972.
```

Note: the first author's name is reversed, for the purpose of alphabetizing; subsequent names appear in their usual order.

¶ BOOK WITH MORE THAN THREE AUTHORS

```
Lauer, Janice M., et al.  Four Worlds of Writing.  2nd ed.
    New York: Harper, 1985.
```

¶ TWO OR MORE WORKS BY THE SAME AUTHOR

```
Parker, John F.  The Independent Writer.  Fort Worth, TX:
    HBJ College Pubs., 1986.

---.  Writing: Processed Product.  Evanston, IL: MacDougal,
    Littell, 1991.
```

Note: to indicate the repeated name, place three hyphens at the left margin followed by a period. If the name refers to an editor or translator, then place

a comma after the hyphens followed by the appropriate abbreviation, e.g.,
`---, ed.`

¶ **BOOK WITH AUTHOR AND EDITOR** (you have quoted the author)

```
Freud, Sigmund.  A General Selection from the Works of
    Sigmund Freud.  Ed. John Rickman.  Garden City, NY:
    Anchor-Doubleday, 1957.
```

Note: when citing the name of a publisher's special imprint—e.g., "Anchor"—give the imprint name first, followed by a hyphen and the publisher's name.

¶ **BOOK WITH AUTHOR AND EDITOR**
(you have quoted the editor's preface)

```
Rickman, John, ed.  Preface.  A General Selection from the
    Works of Sigmund Freud.  By Sigmund Freud.  Garden
    City, NY: Anchor-Doubleday, 1957.
```

¶ **BOOK IN TRANSLATION**

```
Camus, Albert.  "The Myth of Sisyphus" and Other Essays.
    Trans. Justin O'Brien.  New York: Vintage, 1955.
```

¶ **BOOK WITH INTRODUCTION BY ANOTHER AUTHOR**
(you have quoted the introduction)

```
Corcoran, J. X. W. P.  Introduction.  The Celts.  By Nora
    Chadwick.  Harmondsworth, Middlesex: Penguin, 1970.
```

Note: Corcoran's name begins this citation because you quoted his introduction. Note, too, that "Introduction" appears in full with a period after it, and the word "By" precedes the name of the author. Use the same style when you quote from a foreword, afterword, or preface by another author.

¶ **BOOK WITHOUT AUTHOR OR EDITOR**

```
The National Geographic Atlas of the World.  5th ed.
    Washington: Natl. Geographic Soc., 1981.
```

Note: this citation would be alphabetized by title under the letter "N" in the works cited without regard to "The."

¶ **BOOK WITH CORPORATE AUTHOR**
(committee, commission, corporation, council, association, etc.)

```
Council on Economic Priorities.  Star Wars: The Economic
     Fallout.  Cambridge, MA: Ballinger, 1987.
```

Note: "MA" is the abbreviation for Massachusetts. See the *MLA Handbook* for a comprehensive list of abbreviations of geographical names.

¶ **BOOK WITH EDITION STATEMENT**

```
Broadwell, Martin M.  The Supervisor as an Instructor: A
     Guide for Classroom Training.  3rd ed.  Reading, MA:
     Addison-Wesley, 1978.
```

¶ **BOOK IN A SERIES**

```
Kelly, Tom, and G. Harvey Summ.  The Good Neighbors:
     America, Panama, and the 1977 Canal Treaties.  Papers
     in International Studies.  Latin America Series 14.
     Athens, OH: Ohio University Center for International
     Studies, 1988.
```

Note: sometimes a publisher produces several volumes in the same format, dealing with the same general area of research. Each book has its own title but belongs to a series. Include the name of the series and the number in the series if they are indicated, as in the example above. Italicize or underline the book title, but not the series name.

¶ **REPUBLISHED BOOK**

```
Collin, W.E.  The White Savannahs.  Introd. Germaine
     Warkentin.  1936.  Toronto: U of Toronto P, 1975.
```

Note: this book was originally published in 1936. It went out of print and then was republished in 1975. The date of original publication is therefore given immediately before the publishing details for the republished edition. The abbreviation "U" stands for "University," and "P" stands for "Press."

¶ **COLLECTION OR ANTHOLOGY** (you have cited the editors)

```
Cone, Edward T., Joseph Frank, and Edmund Keeley, eds.
     The Legacy of R. P. Blackmur: Essays, Memoirs, Texts.
     New York: Ecco, 1987.
```

Note: the colon here, and in "Book With Edition Statement" above, introduces a subtitle. The subtitle often appears only on the title page, and is sometimes distinguished by a different typeface, but nonetheless you must include it in the full title in works cited.

¶ STORY (OR ESSAY) IN A COLLECTION OR ANTHOLOGY

```
Tyler, Anne.  "Holding Things Together."  In We Are the
     Stories We Tell: The Best Short Stories by North
     American Women Since 1945.  Ed. Wendy Martin.  New
     York: Pantheon, 1990.  150-63.
```

Note: in this example, and in the two that follow, inclusive page numbers for the entire work cited appear at the end of the citation. Use the word "In" before the title to show that the author is one of several; omit this word when the entire collection is by a single author, as in the following example.

```
Illich, Ivan.  "Outwitting Developed Nations."  Toward a
     History of Needs.  New York: Bantam, 1980.  54-67.
```

¶ POEM (STORY, OR ESSAY) IN A MULTIVOLUME COLLECTION OR ANTHOLOGY

```
Rossetti, Christina.  "An Apple Gathering."  In The Norton
     Anthology of English Literature.  Ed. M. H. Abrams et
     al.  4th ed.  2 vols.  New York: Norton, 1979.  2:
     1522-23.
```

Note: the "2" preceding the colon is the volume number.

¶ TWO OR MORE WORKS IN A COLLECTION

```
Gardner, Martin, ed.  Great Essays in Science.  New York:
     Washington Square, 1957.

Krutch, Joseph Wood.  "The Colloid and the Crystal."
     Gardner 106-07.

Russell, Bertrand.  "The Greatness of Albert Einstein."
     Gardner 398-402.
```

Note: to avoid repetition of publishing details when citing two or more different works in a collection, list the collection separately. For individual works referred to in your text, give the author's name, and the title, followed by the editor's last name and the page numbers for the entire work. Thus the name "Gardner" in the last two entries above provides a cross reference to the first entry, which contains the full publishing details.

¶ **REVIEW OF A FILM, PLAY, BOOK, EXHIBITION, ETC.**

```
Corliss, Richard.   "A Vampire With Heart."   Rev. of Bram
     Stoker's Dracula, dir. by Francis Ford Coppola.   Time
     30 Nov. 1992: 69.
```

Note: the abbreviation "dir." for "directed" indicates that a film review is being cited—"by" alone would signify a book title. Here Corliss is the reviewer, and "Rev. of" stands for "Review of." Observe that there is no punctuation between the magazine title and the date, but that a colon, followed by a letter space, goes between the year and the page number. For weekly magazines, the date replaces the volume number, and so is not enclosed in parentheses.

¶ **ARTICLE IN A JOURNAL WITH A VOLUME NUMBER**

```
Meier, Kathryn S.   "Tobacco Truths: The Impact of Role
     Models on Children's Attitudes Toward Smoking."
     Health Education Quarterly 18.2 (Summer 1991): 173-82.
```

Note: journals are scholarly publications appearing monthly, quarterly, or yearly. Magazines usually appear weekly or monthly and are more widely available, often at newsstands. The term "volume" refers to the collection of issues in an annual series.

If a journal begins each new issue with page 1, add a period and the issue number immediately after the volume number—in the example above, 18 is the volume number, and 2 is the issue number. Some libraries shelve journals by date rather than by number, so it is helpful to include the month (or season) and year in a parenthesis, as shown.

If a journal uses an issue number but not a volume number, include it as if it were the volume number.

If a journal has continuous pagination throughout the volume, i.e., does not begin each issue with page 1, give the volume number followed by the year of publication in a parenthesis, a colon, and the inclusive page numbers of the article you cited, as in the following example.

```
Rau, Santha Rama.   "Benares: India's City of Light."
     National Geographic 169 (1986): 215-51.
```

¶ **ARTICLE IN A NEWSPAPER** (unsigned)

```
"Somalia Needs Long-term Help." Seattle Post-
     Intelligencer 6 Dec. 1992: D2.
```

Note: many newspapers paginate by section. In this case provide both section and page, without a space between. When newspaper sections are identified with numbers (instead of letters), use the style shown in the next example. When a newspaper is paginated continuously, give the page number(s) alone.

¶ **ARTICLE IN A NEWSPAPER** (signed)

```
Dowd, Maureen.  "Clinton as National Idol: Can the
     Honeymoon Last?" New York Times 3 Jan. 1993,
     sec. 1: 1.
```

¶ **ARTICLE IN A WEEKLY OR MONTHLY MAGAZINE**

```
"Exit Nixon." Time 19 Aug. 1974: 15-17.

Thomas, Lewis.  "On the AIDS Problem." Discover May 1983:
     42+.
```

Note: the + sign in the above citation shows that the article begins on page 42 but is then interrupted by intervening material.

¶ **ARTICLE IN A REFERENCE WORK** (unsigned)

```
"San Bernardino Mountains." Encyclopedia Americana.
     1991 ed.
```

Note: because encyclopedias usually arrange articles alphabetically throughout, volume and page numbers are omitted. If the work is well known, specify only the edition, if stated, and the year of publication. For less well known reference works, give full publishing details.

```
"(Adeline) Virginia Woolf." Introduction. Twentieth-
     Century Literary Criticism. Vol. 5. 1981. 505-06.
```

Note: here you begin with the title of the entire section on Woolf. You include "Introduction" because you referred to it and not the excerpts that follow it—no author is given. Because the series alphabetizes within each volume and not throughout, you give the volume number. You also include the page numbers for the introduction because it is only part of the section on Woolf.

¶ ARTICLE IN A REFERENCE WORK (signed)

```
Hills, Theo L.  "Great Lakes."  The World Book
    Encyclopedia.  1980 ed.
```

Note: if given, the author's name usually appears at the end of the article. Sometimes articles are signed with initials identified elsewhere in the work.

¶ ARTICLE REPRINTED IN A REFERENCE WORK (signed)

```
Thomas, Clara.  "The Wild Garden and the Manawaka World."
    Modern Fiction Studies 22 (Autumn 1976): 401-12.
    Excerpted under "Laurence, (Jean) Margaret" in
    Contemporary Literary Criticism.  Vol. 13.  1980.
    342-44.
```

Note: you referred to excerpts from Clara Thomas's previously published article. You give the original source first, and then the source you used after the words "Excerpted under." You use the word "Excerpt" because only parts of the original article are reprinted in your source, and "under" because "Laurence, (Jean) Margaret" is the alphabetized title under which the excerpts appear. If the whole article was reprinted, you would use "Rpt." for "Reprinted" instead of "Excerpted." You include page numbers since your source is only part of the section on Laurence.

¶ YEARBOOK, ANNUAL

```
The Europa Year Book 1985: A World Survey.  Vol. 1.
    London: Europa, 1985.
```

¶ CONFERENCE PROCEEDINGS

```
Second National Forum on Handgun Control: Proceedings.
    7-9 Jan. 1976.  Washington: United States Conference
    of Mayors, 1976.
```

¶ ANNUAL REPORT

```
International Joint Commission.  Annual Report on Great
    Lakes Water Quality.  Windsor, ON, 1978.
```

```
Great Britain.  Colonial Office.  Annual Report on the
    Social and Economic Progress of the People of Hong
    Kong.  London, 1938.
```

48

¶ SPECIAL REPORT

Mayor's Bicycle Advisory Council. <u>The Bike 2000 Plan: A</u>
<u>Plan to Make Chicago Bicycle-friendly by the Year</u>
<u>2000</u>. Chicago, 1992.

¶ PAMPHLET

<u>Acid Rain</u>. Society for Promoting Environmental
Conservation (SPEC), n.d.

Note: sometimes pamphlets omit essential details, as here. No author is given or date of publication, hence the abbreviation "n.d." for "no date." But as far as possible, cite a pamphlet as if it were a book.

¶ RESERVE ARTICLE

Roberts, James D. <u>Catholics, Divorce and Remarriage</u>.
Photocopy of text of a lecture to the conference of
the Assn. of Separated and Divorced Catholics,
Toronto, 19 Sept. 1986. Revised 1989. Placed on
library reserve by J. Roberts, Religious Studies Dept.

Note: items placed on reserve are often published books or journal articles. In such cases, cite them in the normal manner, with full publishing details.

Government Sources

Citations for government-issued documents and publications usually begin with the jurisdiction, or government name, which stands in place of an author's name. This may be followed by the relevant department, branch, office, committee or other subdivision(s) of the government structure. The examples shown below cite federal government documents, but the same forms may be employed for citation of state, local and foreign government documents. For more extensive details consult Turabian.

¶ **GOVERNMENT PUBLICATION** (no author given)

```
United States.  Dept. of Labour.  Bureau of Labor
     Statistics.  Brief History of the American Labor
     Movement.  Washington: GPO, 1964.
```

Note: "GPO" is the abbreviation for the United States Government Printing Office, the publisher-of-record for thousands of federal government documents.

```
United States.  National Aeronautics and Space
     Administration.  Advisory Council.  Solar System
     Exploration Committee.  Planetary Exploration Through
     Year 2000: An Augmented Program.  Washington: NASA,
     1986.
```

¶ **GOVERNMENT PUBLICATION** (author or editor given)

```
United States.  Dept. of State.  The United States and
     Russia: The Beginning of Relations, 1765-1815.  Ed.
     Nina N. Bashkina, et al.  Washington: GPO, 1980.
```

Note: use "By" instead of "Ed." when an author's name is given. Or, you may begin the citation with the name of the author or editor. Better still, cross reference the item by author or editor name, as below:

```
Bashkina, Nina N., et al., eds.  1980.  See US Dept. of
     State.  1980.
```

¶ CONGRESSIONAL DEBATE

```
United States. Congress. Senate. Senator Kerry of
    Massachusetts speaking for the International Dolphins
    Conservation Act of 1992, H.R. 5419. 102nd Cong., 2nd
    sess., Congressional Record (8 Oct. 1992), vol. 138,
    no. 144. Daily ed.
```

Note: the *Congressional Record*, published by the GPO, is the official transcript of all the proceedings of both houses of Congress. It appears first in a daily edition; a revised edition is published later in bound volumes and other formats. Be sure to cite the daily edition if it is your source because its pagination is different from the final version. If your essay text provides enough detail and context, a shorter citation with page numbers may be sufficient. This style, shown below, is advised by the *MLA Handbook*. If in doubt, consult your instructor.

```
Cong. Rec.   8 Oct. 1992: S17840-S17843. Daily ed.
```

¶ CONGRESSIONAL COMMITTEE HEARING

```
United States. Congress. Senate. Committee on the
    Judiciary. The Constitutional Roles of Congress and
    the President in Declaring and Waging War: Hearings
    Before the Committee on the Judiciary. 102nd Cong.,
    1st sess., 8 Jan. 1991. Washington: GPO, 1991.
```

¶ CONGRESSIONAL COMMITTEE REPORT

```
United States. Congress. House. Select Committee on
    Aging. Subcommittee on Health and Long-term Care.
    Elder Abuse: A National Disgrace. A report by Rep.
    Claude Pepper, subcommittee chair. 99th Cong., 1st
    sess. Committee print. Washington: GPO, 1985.
```

¶ BILL or RESOLUTION

```
United States. Congress. Senate. Aviation Security
    Improvement Act. 101st Cong., 2nd sess., H.R. 5732.
    Congressional Record. Vol. 136, no. 146. Daily ed.
    (23 Oct. 1990), S16544-S16551.
```

Note: bills and resolutions are numbered alphanumerically. Above, "H.R. 5732" indicates a bill originating in the House of Representatives. "S" would indicate the Senate; "S. J. Res." means Senate Joint Resolution, and so forth.

¶ STATUTE

<u>Iraq Sanctions Act of 1990</u>. <u>Statutes At Large</u>. Vol. 104,
    part 3, sec. 586 (1990). Washington: GPO, 1990.

Note: once passed into law, bills and joint resolutions are called statutes, and are published by the GPO in annual editions of *Statutes At Large*. Statutes also become part of the United States Code, which the GPO updates and publishes at six-year intervals. The code is organized by "title," with sections within each title. A short-form citation begins with the title number but is alphabetized under "United States Code." A more detailed form of citation, including statute name, may be preferred. Samples of both follow. Choose one style and be consistent.

42 <u>U.S. Code</u>. Secs. 7401-7641. 1988.

<u>Clean Air Act</u>. <u>United States Code</u>. Title 42, secs.
    7401-7641 (Vol. 17, 1988). Washington: GPO, 1988.

¶ TREATY

United States. Dept. of State. "Treaty Between the
    United States of America and the Union of Soviet
    Socialist Republics on the Limitation of
    Anti-Ballistic Missile Systems," 26 May 1972.
    TIAS no. 7503. <u>United States Treaties and Other
    International Agreements</u>, vol. 23, pt. 4.

Note: "TIAS" stands for "Treaties and other International Acts," a series of State Department pamphlets which are compiled and published by the GPO in the above cited reference work.

¶ UNITED STATES CONSTITUTION

Note: citations of the Constitution can be handled with parenthetical references in the text of your essay (see page 38).

Nonprint Sources

For most nonprint sources it is necessary to identify the medium. For audiotapes, videotapes, phonograph records, compact disks, slide programs, film strips, microforms, computer software, and interviews, name the medium immediately after the title. For motion pictures, radio and television programs, and works of art, name the medium only if it is not clear from the title of the work or the other information given in the citation.

¶ **TELEVISION PROGRAM**

> Cat On a Hot Tin Roof. By Tennessee Williams. Dir. Jack
>> Hofiss. American Playhouse. PBS. KCTS/9, Seattle.
>> 31 July 1985.

Note: the series title, American Playhouse, appears after the program reference, and is not underlined or put in quotation marks. PBS is the network, and KCTS/9 is the broadcast station.

¶ **RADIO PROGRAM**

> Fresh Air. NPR. KPLU-FM, Tacoma. 4 March 1993.

Note: NPR (National Public Radio) is the network; KPLU is the local broadcast station.

¶ **MOTION PICTURE**

> Welles, Orson, dir. Citizen Kane. With Welles and Joseph
>> Cotten. RKO, 1941.

Note: Welles and Cotten are identified as principal actors. Other individuals may be mentioned when relevant to your text, e.g., producer, screenwriter, film score composer, etc. If you have emphasized the film rather than the director in your text, the title should appear first with the director's name following.

¶ **RECORDING** (phonograph record, audiotape, compact disk)

> Chapman, Tracy. "Woman's Work." Matters of the Heart.
>> Compact disk. Electra Entertainment, CD61215, 1992.

Note: the disk number (or album or tape number) appears after the name of the recording company.

```
Ellington, Duke.  "A Tone Parallel to Harlem (The Harlem
     Suite)."  1951.  Uptown.  Audiotape.  CBS, WCT40836,
     n.d.
```

Note: the above audiotape is a re-release of previously recorded material. The tape's liner notes indicate 1951 as the original recording date. No date is given for the issue of this tape, hence "n.d."

¶ VIDEOTAPE

```
The Human Experiment.  Videocassette.  Ethics in America
     Series 9.  Santa Barbara: Intellimation, 1989.
     58 min.
```

Note: state the running time of the tape, after the date and the name of the distributor.

¶ SLIDE PROGRAM

```
Learning by All Means.  Slide program.  Media and Library
     Association and California Audio Visual Education
     Distributors Association, n.d.  38 slides.
```

Note: "n.d." indicates no date is given for the issue of this slide program. If a date is given, include it. State the number of slides in the program, after the date.

¶ FILMSTRIP

```
Michelangelo: The Sistine Chapel.  Filmstrip.  Life
     Filmstrips, 1950.  62 frames.
```

Note: state the length of the filmstrip, in number of frames, after the date.

¶ WORK OF ART

```
Van Gogh, Vincent.  Starry Night.  Museum of Modern Art,
     New York.
```

Note: underline the title of a sculpture, a painting, or any other "published" work of art.

¶ **MICROFORM** (microfilm, microfiche, microprint, etc.)

```
Richardson, Penelope L.   Issues in Television-centered
     Instruction.   Microfiche.   Bethesda, MD.: ERIC
     Document Reproduction Services, ED 205 217, 1981.
```

Note: include the name of the medium after the title for a work originally published in microform. Omit the name of a microform medium used to store a previously published printed work, and cite the work as if it were the original.

¶ **COMPUTER SOFTWARE**

```
Microsoft Access: Relational Database Managment System for
     Windows.   Computer software.   Microsoft Corporation,
     1992.   Windows 3.0, 2MB, disk.
```

Note: if an author is given, begin with the author. After the date, include the operating system which the software requires, the units of memory needed, and the form of the program—in this case "disk."

¶ **INTERVIEW**

```
Prince, Linda.   Personal interview.   2 Aug. 1991.
```

Note: personal interviews should be distinguished from telephone interviews. In general, an interview has weight only when you are citing an authority—someone with informed opinions. Indicate his or her credentials in your text: College librarian Linda Prince said that. . . . See the *MLA Handbook* for how to document interviews from magazines, radio, or television.

¶ **SPEECH**

```
Freeman, Roger A.   "Does America Neglect Its Poor?"
     Speech delivered to Stanford Alumni Assn.   Stanford
     San Francisco Women's Club.   San Francisco, 14 March
     1990.
```

The APA Style of Documentation

The influential American Psychological Association (APA) advocates a somewhat different system both for indicating sources of paraphrases, summaries, and quotations in the text of the essay and for listing references at the end. With minor variations, the social sciences (Psychology, Anthropology, and Sociology) and some physical sciences (e.g., Biology) employ the APA conventions outlined here.

Below is a sample page from a long article recently accepted for publication. It illustrates several major features of APA style including page format, a variety of typical references for paraphrase and summary, and the use of direct quotations. The writer uses APA software that will paginate, print running heads, and help build a proper list of works cited. Student papers may not require page headings. Consult your instructor.

Page Format

1. APA title page layout is the same as that in the sample (page 9).
2. A running head appears flush right in the upper right corner of every page, one inch from the top. The heading is identical to the essay title, if brief, or is a shortened form of a long title.
3. The page number appears on all pages, starting with the title page, one double space below the heading, again at the right-hand margin.
4. The text begins one double space below the page number.

Text References

1. Parenthetical references do not contain titles.
2. When you use paraphrase or summary and refer to the author in your sentence, the parenthesis contains only the date of publication.
3. When you use paraphrase or summary without mentioning the author in the sentence, your reference should include the author(s), followed by a comma, and the date.
4. Use an ampersand (&) instead of "and" for two authors in a parenthetical reference: "(Webster & Young, 1988)".
5. When you quote an author whose name is in your sentence, provide the date in parentheses immediately after the name, and a page reference (using "p." or "pp.") directly after the quotation and before the sentence period. (See the last sentence of the first paragraph of the sample page.)

Sample APA Style Text Page

In terms of the clinical/reminiscence domain
there has been an emerging emphasis on the distinction
between "historical truth" and "narrative truth" (Bru-
ner, 1986; Spence, 1984). The former connotes a static
reservoir of directly (although not necessarily easily)
retrievable and unimpeachable "facts"; the latter
explicitly acknowledges the reconstructive and dynamic
nature of memory recall and is more concerned with its
verisimilitude than with documentable accuracy. Within
the parameters of narrative truth, clinicians and
clients jointly facilitate the retrieval and elucida-
tion of memories which form a life portrait supported
by current self-structures (e.g., Webster & Young,
1988). This is a dynamic process leading to narrative
revisions, defined by Bonanno (1990) as ". . . the
re-evaluation or re-experiencing of the past in the
context of a new conceptual framework" (p. 176).

In terms of autobiographical memories, McAdams
(1989) demonstrated that personality factors (i.e.,
themes of intimacy and power) were strongly associated
with autobiographical memories of "peak experiences."
Specifically, themes of intimacy or power were higher
in peak experience protocols of subjects who had correspondingly high themes on prior projective personality

6. When you quote without indicating the author in your text, the reference after the quotation is as follows:

```
" . . . narrative revisions" (Webster, 1991, p. 65).
```

7. If two or more works by the same author were published in the same year, distinguish between them in references by coding each with lower-case "a," "b," "c," etc., in order of their appearance in your list of works cited:

```
Bonanno (1988b) proposes that the true . . .
```

8. If more than one source has contributed to the content of a summary or paraphrase, arrange them in alphabetical order by author; include the dates, and use a semicolon to separate them:

```
(Bruner, 1986; Spence, 1984)
```

Using Notes in APA Style

Content or informational notes use the same conventions as for MLA note style (see page 11).

Bibliographical Citations

Though a list of works cited and a list of references in APA style are identical in many respects, there are important differences. As with any style, the APA is strict about the order and form of the parts of an entry.

1. Begin a fresh page (continuing the pagination of the text) by centering the word "References" one inch from the top.
2. Each entry begins at the left margin; subsequent lines are indented three letter spaces.
3. Double-space throughout the list.
4. For more than one author, all names appear in reverse order (not just the first); give all surnames in full, others in initials only; use "&" instead of "and" before the last name. Note: in a text reference, if there are more than six authors mention only the first, using "et al." for the others.
5. List two or more works by the same author(s) in chronological order (earliest publication first), spelling out the author's full name in each entry.
6. Place a period after each major part of an entry.
7. Following the author(s), place the date in a parenthesis—hence the term "author-date" system.
8. If you have used two or more works published in the same year by the same author or co-authors, code the dates in succession with "a" then "b" then "c"; insert a period when the parenthesis is complete.

9. Next comes the title of the book or article. For a book, underline title (and subtitle), and capitalize only the first word of title (and subtitle); for an article, do not use quotation marks or underlining, and capitalize as for a book title, including all proper names. (Do *not* italicize in place of underlining in APA style.)
10. City and publisher, linked by a colon, precede the final period (e.g., second model entry).
11. The name of a journal, using upper- and lower-case letters, is underlined. A comma separates it from the volume number (in arabic numerals, without "vol."), which is also underlined (e.g., last entry).
12. If volumes of a journal are numbered continuously, provide inclusive page numbers for the article, without "pp." (e.g., last entry).
13. If each issue in a volume is numbered separately, include the issue number in a parenthesis following the volume number (e.g., first entry).
14. If the article is from an edited collection or anthology, the word "In" introduces the name of the editor(s), followed by "ed." or "eds." plus a comma, and then the book title (underlined). Inclusive page numbers follow directly in a parenthesis (no punctuation precedes), with "pp." to indicate "pages" (e.g., third entry).

Documenting Research in Sociology

Essays in Sociology follow the basic APA guidelines given above, with a few differences:

TEXT REFERENCES
1. No comma after the author(s).
2. Parenthetical references usually include page numbers.
3. No "p." or "pp." in parentheses. Typical references:

    (Giddens 1987, 15); (Giddens 1979c, 37-38)

WORKS CITED
1. The list may be labeled either "References" or "Works Cited."
2. The position of the year of publication may be in either MLA or APA style.

Consult the section on APA style above for all other matters of form. For further guidance, ask your instructor for models or imitate the conventions used in currently published articles in the field. Ultimately, instructors are almost universally agreed that the greatest virtue in your documentation style ought to be *consistency*.

Documenting Research in Biology

Biology essays use APA (author-date) conventions, with some exceptions:

TEXT REFERENCES

1. For two authors, use "and" not "&" in the parenthesis:

   `(Smith and Jones, 1991).`

2. Place a comma after the author(s).
3. Quotations are generally not used.
4. If you must quote or indicate a specific page from a book, the page number follows the date and a colon, without "p." or "pp.":

   `The Indole test was performed to isolate Salmonella from Edwardsiella (Barnett, 1988: 380); a negative result confirmed Salmonella.`

5. As shown above, references usually appear inside your sentences, as close as possible to the material you have used.
6. In order to show that several consecutive pieces of information in your paragraph have the same source, place the reference at the end, after the sentence period:

   `. . . and confirmed that Salmonella usually produces hydrogen sulfide. (Sneath, 1984: 415)`

   Note: in both references and citations, Latin names for species are underlined.

WORKS CITED

1. The list of works cited is headed with "Literature Cited" or "References."
2. Include names of all authors, spelling out the last names only and using initials for first and middle names.
3. Following the author(s) comes the year of publication, standing alone without parentheses.
4. Write out the complete title of an article, without quotation marks and capitalizing only the first word:

   `Singer, S. J., and G. Nicholson. 1972. Fluid mosaic model of the structure of cell membranes. Science 175: 720.`

5. Abbreviate complex journal names but not one-word names.
6. Following the volume number (without "vol.") of a journal, a colon precedes the inclusive page numbers given in full:

   `Marine Biol. 85: 157-166.`

7. In citing a book title, indicate volume number, if any (include "Vol."),
   publishing information, and pages consulted (include "pp."):

```
Laskin, A. I., and H. A. Lechevalier, eds. 1973. CRC
    Handbook of Systematic Microbiology. Vol. 2. Williams
    and Williams, Baltimore, MD., pp. 118-124.
```

Note: the publisher precedes the place, and there is a comma between
them.

Sample APA Style References

References

87

```
Bonanno, G. A. (1990). Remembering and psychotherapy.
    Psychotherapy, 27(2), 175-186.
Bruner, J. (1986). Actual minds, possible worlds.
    Cambridge, MA: Harvard University Press.
McAdams, D. P. (1989). The development of a narrative
    identity. In D. M. Buss, & N. Cantor (eds.),
    Personality psychology: Recent trends and emerg-
    ing directions. New York: Springer-Verlag.
Spence, D. P. (1984). Narrative truth and historical
    truth. New York: Norton.
Webster, J. D., & Young, R. A. (1988). Process
    variables of the life review: Counselling
    implications. International Journal of Aging and
    Human Development, 26, 315-323.
```

The Note Style of Documentation

Although parenthetical text-referencing systems of documentation are widely used, in some classes you may still be expected to use numbered footnotes or endnotes to acknowledge sources. Many books and articles employ this traditional method, so you should familiarize yourself with its basic conventions, in any case.

Ask your instructor whether you should use footnotes or endnotes. In general, the more notes you have, the more practical it is to gather them together as endnotes at the end of the text.

Placement of Notes and Note Numbers

In the note system, quotations, paraphrases, and other uses of source material are numbered consecutively from [1] throughout the text with arabic superscripts (numbers that go a half space above the line, as shown above). They are then acknowledged in correspondingly numbered notes that appear either at the foot of the text pages, or on a separate page (or pages) under the heading "Notes" immediately following the end of the text.

Good word-processing programs will help you create footnotes and endnotes, handling the placing of superscript numbers and the spacing of lines. If you use such a program, obviously you must accept its conventions.

The guidelines below follow both MLA style and Turabian.

1. Place a superscript number in your text immediately following any phrase, clause, or sentence that contains quoted, paraphrased, or summarized material.
2. Place the number outside any final punctuation (except a dash).
3. Leave a letter space after the number but not in front of it.
4. Do not punctuate the number in any way.
5. Match this text number to a footnote number (superscript) at the bottom of the page, or to an endnote number (superscript) on a separate page at the end of the text.
6. Write the note after the appropriate note number.

See the following model of part of an essay showing the placement of numbers in the text and the corresponding footnotes.

Content of First Notes

For the first reference to a book give full details. Include in the note the author's full name as given on the title page, the title (including subtitle, if any), the name of an editor or translator (if any), the volume and edition numbers (if any), the city of publication, the publisher's name, the date of publication, and the page number of the reference. Provide corresponding information for other works—see the sample entries that follow.

The convention used to be that if a bibliographical detail—most commonly the author's name—appeared in the text, it was not repeated in the note. However, Turabian sensibly rules that the author's name must appear in the note, regardless of whether it is a first note or a subsequent note (except when ibid. is used).

Note Layout

1. Begin footnotes three line spaces below the text. Separate the notes from the text with a 2-inch line (to create it, hit the underline key twenty times) beginning at the left margin one line space below the text. Begin the notes two line spaces below that line.
2. Indent the first line of a note five letter spaces from the left margin; begin subsequent lines at the margin.
3. Single space footnotes, but double space endnotes. Double space between entries in both footnotes and endnotes.
4. Leave one letter space between the superscript number and the beginning of the note.
5. First and last names of authors appear in the normal order.
6. Place a comma between the author's name and the title of the work, and between the publisher's name and the date of publication. Put parentheses around the city of publication, the publisher, and the year of publication. Place a colon followed by one letter space between the city of publication and the publisher's name. Be sure to put a period at the end of the entry. Leave only one letter space between major parts of the note.
7. Do *not* use the abbreviations "p.", "pp." or "pg." before the page number.

Subsequent Notes

The first time you acknowledge a source, provide full details, as indicated above. For all subsequent references to the same source, use one of the abbreviated forms of the note described below.

SUCCESSIVE REFERENCES

When references to a particular source follow one another immediately, with no other reference intervening, use "ibid." (an abbreviation of the Latin *ibidem* meaning "in the same place") instead of repeating the whole note.

Add only those details that are different in the new note—usually a page number. Note 13 on the sample page is a second reference to the same page in the same work by May, noted immediately above. If this note referred to another page in May's work, page 43 for example, it would read, "Ibid., 43."

SEPARATED REFERENCES

When references to a particular source are separated by other references, use the author's last name alone in the subsequent note, together with the page number (whether different or not). Thus in note 16 on the sample page, the name "Seymour" refers the reader to note 14 and the work entitled "America Enters the War."

If you had referred to two works by Seymour, then you would distinguish between them in the subsequent note by including an abbreviated form of the title: [16] Seymour, "America," 57.

Note Terms and Abbreviations

The traditional footnote method employed Latin abbreviations to indicate subsequent references. The *MLA Handbook* and Turabian both recommend against their continued use, preferring the simple repetition of an author's last name, plus a page number. But since they appear in already published works, you should understand their meaning:

loc. cit. (*loco citato*)
means "in the place (or passage) cited," i.e., in the same passage referred to in a nearby note. It is preceded by an author's name, in the note or in the text, but is not followed by a page number since the passage has already been identified in the previous note.

op. cit. (*opere citato*)
means "in the work cited." It is used when referring to a passage on a different page of a work noted nearby. Again it is preceded by an author's name in note or text, but this time a new page number appears.

Two Latin terms are, however, still widely used in the note system of documentation. One has been mentioned above, "ibid.," which is used to refer to the work mentioned in the immediately preceding note. Another is "passim," meaning "here and there." Use it in a note together with page numbers or a chapter number to indicate that the material referred to is scattered throughout a particular section of the text: e.g., "60-95 passim" or "chap. 3 passim." The abbreviation "et al." (*et alii*), meaning "and others," may be used when you refer in a note to a work with more than three authors. (Turabian prefers "and others"—also acceptable.)

5

frequently in the past."[12] On February 26, however, the Cunard liner _Laconia_ was sunk.[13] The sinking of the _Algonquin_ followed on March 12; and then, on March 19, word arrived of the sinking of three American ships within a space of twenty-four hours.[14] As other options disappeared, the President realized that "his choice lay between acquiescing in the German submarine campaign or calling upon Congress for a declaration of war."[15] He chose the latter course.

It is sometimes claimed that President Wilson's decision was unduly influenced by interest groups acting for the allies. Charles Seymour disputes this view saying,

> There is no scrap of valid evidence supporting this thesis, and all that is available directly controverts it. At the beginning of the war Wilson declared and believed that it could not touch us, that if we kept clean neutral hands we were fulfilling our duty and preserving our security. He was speedily disabused.[16]

In the face of the submarine attacks, all the President's

---

[12] Ernest R. May, ed., _The Coming of War, 1917_, The Berkeley Series in American History (Chicago: Rand McNally, 1963), 41.

[13] Ibid.

[14] Charles Seymour, "America Enters the War," in _Intervention, 1917: Why America Fought_, ed. Warren I. Cohen, Problems in American Civilization Series (Boston: Heath, 1966), 56.

[15] May, 48.

[16] Seymour, 57.

Works Cited

A list of works cited may not be needed, especially if you have already listed your notes as endnotes at the end of the text. Ask your instructor. If a works cited list is necessary, follow the guidelines set out on pages 39-41.

Sample Notes

¶ BOOK WITH ONE AUTHOR

¹ Jackson J. Benson, <u>The True Adventures of John Steinbeck, Writer</u> (New York: Viking, 1984), 658.

Note: punctuate notes with commas except in front of a parenthesis.

¶ BOOK WITH MORE THAN THREE AUTHORS

² Gail S. Goodman, et al., <u>Testifying in Criminal Court: Emotional Effects on Child Sexual Assault Victims</u> (Chicago: U of Chicago P, 1992), 79.

¶ BOOK WITH EDITOR

³ Robert Bartlett Haas, ed., <u>Reflection on the Atom Bomb: Volume 1 of the Previously Uncollected Writings of Gertrude Stein</u> (Los Angeles: Black Sparrow, 1973), 139.

¶ ESSAY IN A COLLECTION

⁴ Robert Audi, "Rationality and Religious Commitment," in <u>Faith, Reason, and Skepticism</u>, ed. Marcus Hester (Philadelphia: Temple UP, 1992), 52.

¶ ARTICLE IN A JOURNAL WITH A VOLUME NUMBER

⁵ Fred I. Greenstein, and R. H. Immerman, "What Did Eisenhower Tell Kennedy About Indochina? The Politics of Misperception," <u>Journal of American History</u> 79 (Sept. 1992), 568-87.

Note: in this journal, pagination is continuous within each volume, so the issue number is omitted. If each issue of a journal is paginated separately, put a period after the volume number and add the issue number, e.g., 79.2. Add the date of issue in parentheses after the volume number. The page numbers at the end refer to the whole article.

¶ ARTICLE IN A WEEKLY OR MONTHLY MAGAZINE

[6] Roger Rosenblatt, "What Really Mattered? Not Just Great Events But Underlying Causes," _Time_, 5 Oct. 1983, 22-25.

[7] Kishu Singh, and Dilip Bobb, "Perishtroika, Mon Amour," _New Internationalist_, Sept. 1990, 20.

Note: identify magazines by date alone; omit volume and issue numbers.

¶ ARTICLE IN A NEWSPAPER (UNSIGNED)

[8] "Piecemeal Parity: Women's Progress Toward Equal Wages is Uneven," _Sunday Oregonian_, 3 Jan. 1993, B2.

¶ ARTICLE IN AN ENCYCLOPEDIA (SIGNED)

[9] Donald MacGillivray Nicol, "Byzantine Empire," _Encyclopaedia Britannica: Macropaedia_, 1974 ed.

Note: this article is signed at the end with initials only. To find the name of the author, look up "D.M.N." in the volume entitled _Propaedia: Guide to the Britannica_. To find the article, look up the alphabetized title. Because articles are alphabetized throughout the work, volume and page numbers are omitted.

¶ CONGRESSIONAL DEBATE

[10] United States, Congress, Senate, H.R. 5419, 102nd Cong., 2nd sess., _Congressional Record_, vol. 138, no. 144, daily ed. (8 Oct. 1992), S17840-S17843.

Index